110648397

SOVIET AND CHINESE COMMUNIST POWER IN THE WORLD TODAY

SOVIET AND CHINESE COMMUNIST POWER IN THE WORLD TODAY

EDITED BY RODGER SWEARINGEN

BASIC BOOKS, INC., PUBLISHERS
NEW YORK / LONDON

Library of Congress Catalog Card Number: 66-29266
Manufactured in the United States of America
BOOK DESIGN BY VINCENT TORRE

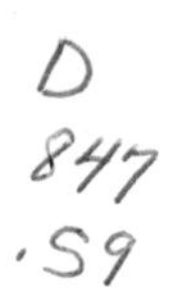

This book is dedicated by its five authors to the late Charles Malamuth, scholar, long-time public servant, journalist, teacher, and good friend of all who came to know him. At the time of his death, in July 1965, Charles Malamuth was Senior Research Associate of the Research Institute on Communist Strategy and Propaganda, School of International Relations, University of Southern California.

The Charles Malamuth Memorial Lectures presented at the University of Southern California in the Spring of 1966, as expanded and updated, form the basis of this volume.

THE AUTHORS

MAX FRANKEL

As diplomatic correspondent of the Washington Bureau of *The New York Times,* Max Frankel brings to his task an extensive background of on-the-spot observation and reporting of events bearing on the Communist world. He has served in Moscow, Cuba, Austria; as an observer of the 1956 Hungarian revolution, the United Nations, and the Geneva Disarmament Conference of 1962. As author, reporter, and television commentator he combines the analytical inquisitiveness of a scholar with the newsman's ability to place current events in context and broad perspective.

PHILIP E. MOSELY

Director of the European Institute of Columbia University and Associate Dean of International Affairs, Professor Mosely heads an extensive program of training and research. From 1942 to 1946, he served the Department of State in intensive planning for the postwar settlements and took part in wartime negotiations with Russia, Britain, and France on problems dealing with the future of Europe. From 1951 to 1955, Dr. Mosely was Director of the Russian Institute, Columbia University. He was also Director of Studies at the Council on Foreign Relations, from 1955 to 1963, where he was in charge of research on foreign policy issues. He is the author of several books on Soviet affairs; the most widely used is perhaps *The Kremlin and World Politics.*

GEORGE E. TAYLOR

Dr. Taylor is Chairman of the Department of Far Eastern and Slavic Languages and Director of the Far Eastern and Russian Institute of the University of Washington. Before World War II he studied in China and even spent some time as an observer with the Chinese Red Army. During the war, Professor Taylor was Deputy Director of the Office of War Information and during 1945–1946 he served as Director of the Office of Information and Cultural Relations for the Far East in the Department of State. He is the author of several books, including *The Struggle for North China*; *The Philippines and the United States*; and, with Franz Michael, *The Far East in the Modern World.*

MARSHALL SHULMAN

Professor of International Politics at the Fletcher School of Law and Diplomacy, Tufts University, and Research Associate at the Russian Research Center at Harvard, Dr. Shulman, a former Special Assistant to the Secretary of State, combines governmental, academic, and newspaper experience in his background of Communist affairs. He has also served as an Information Officer of the U.S. Mission to the United Nations. His latest book, *Beyond the Cold War,* supplements his 1963 book, *Stalin's Foreign Policy Reappraised.* Dr. Shulman is a former President of the American Association for the Advancement of Slavic Studies.

RODGER SWEARINGEN

Dr. Swearingen is Professor of International Relations and Director of the Research Institute on Communist Strategy and Propaganda at the University of Southern California. His specialty is Soviet and Chinese Communist foreign policy. He has served as consultant with the Department of State, the U.S. Air Force, the RAND Corporation, the Asia Foundation, and the Ford Foundation. His books and publications include the text *The World of Communism* and *What's So Funny, Comrade?*; he is editor of *Focus World Communism* and co-author of *Red Flag in Japan: International Communism in Action.* He has traveled extensively in the Soviet Union and Eastern Europe and has undertaken three fact-finding tours to Vietnam and the Far East since 1964.

PREFACE

I

Before the ink was dry on the surrender documents ending World War II with the total defeat of Germany, Italy, and Japan, the United States found itself conspicuously confronted by a new aggressor — the Soviet Union. The initial, improvised American response took the form of the Truman Doctrine for Greece and Turkey and the Marshall Plan for Europe, twin countermeasures soon linked and elaborated into an over-all United States policy called "containment." George Kennan, former American Ambassador to Moscow, will be remembered as the "Mr. X" whose article, "The Sources of Soviet Conduct," in *Foreign Affairs*, July 1947, first publicly enunciated the policy and its rationale — a policy which was to govern the turbulent course of U.S. relations with the Communist world during the next several postwar years. Kennan assessed the nature of the problem and pointed to the evident need for containment. "It is clear," he said, "that the United States cannot expect in the foreseeable future to enjoy political intimacy with the Soviet regime. It must continue to regard the Soviet Union as a rival, not a partner, in the political arena. It must continue to expect that Soviet policies will reflect no abstract love of peace and stability, no real faith in the possibility of a permanent happy coexistence of the socialist and capitalist worlds, but rather a cautious, persistent pressure towards the disruption and weakening of all rival influence and rival power."

During the Truman and Eisenhower years, 1945–1960, the United States found itself in regular and serious conflict with the Soviet Union and, after 1950, with Communist China as well. These two allied nations of World War II had become the adversaries. A calculated Communist strategy of probing and pushing, of creating incidents of infiltration and subversion, of promoting revolution, and even of "naked aggression" (as President Truman called the war in Korea) — this persistent Communist policy on the part of both Moscow and Peking fills the archives and annals of history. The record of the first postwar decade and a half furnished little cause for optimism over the prospects of improving relations with the Communist world. Some of the more serious incidents include the Soviet attempt to subvert Greece and Turkey (1946), the Communist uprisings in Southeast Asia (1947–1948), the Soviet take-over of Czechoslovakia and the Berlin Blockade (1948), the Communist-initiated Korean War (1950), the Chinese Communist intervention in Korea (1951), the Chinese Communist conquest of Tibet (1951), the incorporation of North Vietnam into the Communist empire (1954), the Kremlin's ruthless suppression of the Hungarian Revolution (1956), the Communist attempt to take over Laos (1957–), and the Communist take-over of Cuba (1960).

Neither the death of Secretary of State John Foster Dulles and his "Brink of War" and "roll back" doctrines nor the replacement of the Eisenhower Republican administration with the Democratic administration of President Kennedy (both events were applauded by the Soviet press) substantially altered the fundamental Soviet antagonism or made it any easier to resolve the basic issues between the U.S. and the U.S.S.R. The "spirit of Camp David" proved as fragile as did the "Hundred Flowers."

In his State of the Union address in January of 1961, President Kennedy acknowledged the West's continuing confrontation with communism. "Our greatest challenge," he said, "... is the world that lies beyond the cold war — but the first great obstacle is still our relations with the Soviet Union and Communist China. We must never be lulled into believing that either power has yielded its ambitions for world domination —

ambitions which they forcefully restated only a short time ago."

U.S. Ambassador to the U.N. Adlai Stevenson underlined the same point when he called attention to the unbroken record of Soviet aggression as well as to Moscow's unaltered aim "to make all the world Communist" and then added that "The world welcomed the process known as de-Stalinization and the movement toward a more normal life within the Soviet Union." "But," Ambassador Stevenson concluded, "the world has not yet seen comparable changes in Soviet foreign policy."

Events of the five years since — the Cuban missile crisis, the Chinese Communist attack on India, stepped up Communist aggression in Vietnam, the increasing intensity of Moscow-Peking disaffection — make it necessary to examine with greatest care the documentation and conclusions of those who see our relations with Moscow as "having improved markedly" as well as the assertion that we are "on a collision course with China." To be sure, the past few years have seen some mellowing in Moscow and great changes within the Communist world — and within our own. The question is: What has changed and what has not?

II

A number of theories have been put forward in an effort to explain the basic aims and character of Soviet and Chinese foreign policies over the decades. In the case of the Soviet Union, two major schools of thought lay claim to the truth of the matter. The first, the power politics school, says the Soviet policy is no more than an extension of tsarist imperialism, the usual manifestations of a major autocratic or totalitarian power. Against this argument, another school of thought insists that it is the ideology that is overriding, that Soviet policy can only be explained in terms of its Marxist-Leninist assumptions, assumptions which comprise, in effect, the operational code of the Politburo. There are also less central theories, such as the Russian search for warm water ports and the great man theory.

Since these theories are not necessarily mutually exclusive, the question becomes one of emphasis. What is the principal motivation of the Kremlin leadership? What does Moscow regard as essential? Does Soviet policy differ fundamentally from the policy of other totalitarian nations or, for that matter, from the traditional British or American approach to foreign affairs? How does the rise to power of a Communist regime in China alter the picture?

The emergence of a Bolshevik, or Communist, government in Russia in 1917 represents a watershed in foreign relations, the initiation of a new kind of foreign policy with no historical precedent. Two fundamental differences distinguish Communist foreign policy from all foreign policies of the modern nations in the eighteenth and nineteenth centuries. The first critical difference is the assumed nonpermanence of the non-Communist government. The second is the replacement, or augmentation, of the traditional practice of government to government relations with a new Communist concept, "peoples' diplomacy." This latter approach became, in practice, a direct appeal to the peoples of the world to support Soviet policies and to work actively for the creation in each country of the world of a Soviet or Communist form of government.

What are the implications for U.S. policy of the great changes going on today within a Communist world in flux? To what extent has Soviet foreign policy since Khrushchev changed fundamentally? What are the aims and special characteristics of Chinese Communist foreign policy? Are relations between Washington and Peking likely to improve — or worsen? To what extent and in what areas are United States relations with the Soviet Union improving? What does the future hold? Are there real prospects for a détente between Washington and Moscow? How serious is the dispute between Moscow and Peking and what are its implications for Asia, for the United States, and for the world? Does Peking simply speak loudly but carry a small stick?

As it happens, 1967 marks the fiftieth anniversary of the advent of modern communism, the Bolshevik Revolution. By

1969 (barring the unexpected), the Communists will have been in power in China for twenty years. How much do we know? What have we learned? And, as Lenin asked, "What is to be done?"

III

To place Soviet and Chinese Communist strategy in perspective and to assess the implications for the West, five senior specialists on foreign policy and Communist affairs bring to bear on the problem a wide range of professional experience and, most significantly, several divergent viewpoints. Four of the authors are directors or former directors of major university centers or institutes on Russian, Far Eastern, or Communist affairs — two on the East Coast and two in the West — Harvard University, Columbia University, the University of Washington and the University of Southern California. The fifth author is a former Moscow correspondent for *The New York Times*, presently *Times* Washington correspondent.

All of the authors combine academic backgrounds with governmental service, journalistic experience, or both, and each has traveled widely in Russia, China, and/or Eastern Europe. Finally, all of the authors have spent their lives in teaching, research, writing, and consulting in the field of foreign policy and of Soviet, Chinese, and Communist affairs.

This volume, then, represents the considered judgments, a summing up by five scholars who have devoted their professional lives to the serious study of the nature and implications of Soviet and Chinese Communist ideology and power in the world of yesterday, today, and tomorrow.

Los Angeles
August 1966

RODGER SWEARINGEN

CONTENTS

SOVIET AND CHINESE COMMUNIST POWER IN THE WORLD TODAY

THE COMMUNIST WORLD IN FLUX

MAX FRANKEL

No discussion of change in the Communist world or any other part of the world ought to begin without some words about our concepts of political and international change.

Change is often discussed by journalists, diplomats, and even by academicians, as if it occurred in fits and starts. We are all victims of the glamour and drama of Chou En-lai walking out on a Moscow party congress or of landlord de Gaulle evicting our NATO offices from Paris. These bits of histrionics are important, and not only because they sell newspapers or bring home on a popular level what scholars and students smugly think they know anyway. Governments — not only newspapers — react to major events, and that gives them great importance.

But I would urge that considerations of change in the world employ the kind of wisdom that begins with the realization that change is constant, whether we detect it or not, and worldwide in its implications.

For years now it has been evident that Communist China and France have felt the two big power blocs in the world to be too constraining. They have been working to free themselves of the discipline of association with more powerful allies whose policies they could not, in the end, dictate or even significantly influence.

So they have cast themselves in the roles of wreckers or spoilers, trying to chip away the bonds of the two blocs. They justify this partial break-up by arguing that Moscow and Washington are too selfish to defend the interests of their allies unless these happen at times to coincide with their own. But the paradox of this particular great and current change on the international scene lies in the fact that Paris and Peking would not dare to break away if the superpowers had not persuaded them (and much of the rest of the world) that they are not likely to plunge everyone into war or to resort to force to hold their empires together.

This process of mutual persuasion between Moscow and Washington is another great stimulus to change, and it, too, is ambivalent. For it consists of a delicate combination of military and technical threat and of tacit diplomatic understanding. It is no accident that Paris and Peking are the two newest members of the nuclear club and that they have failed to sign the test-ban treaty. The monopolistic possession of nuclear weapons has been a major instrument of Soviet and American domination of their respective alliances. One path to freedom and bargaining power, therefore, lies in breaking that monopoly.

To ambivalence and paradox is added the irony that missile technology has helped Paris and Peking and the other lesser allies of the Big Two to find more freedom of maneuver as they chip away at the Big Two. Their own territories have become less and less necessary to the military postures of the Soviet Union and the United States, and neither of the Big Two would now shed blood to hang on to the territorial extensions that alliance with others, especially in Europe, once made possible. Feeling less needed, the smaller Communist and non-Communist nations of Europe might eventually come to feel less safe;

but for the moment they feel more free to pursue their own economic and diplomatic objectives than they did when they were on the front lines of a very rigorous cold war.

All this has not given us a very secure system of peace guarantees, but another technical fact, the very horror of modern weapons, has made it credible to the players of world diplomacy.

Raymond Aron of France has said that one of the most formidable alliances in the world today is the alliance of Washington and Moscow against war between themselves. It does not imply the end of conflict between them, but it does mean that each is prepared to forego or even to sacrifice some of its important objectives to preserve that compact. We held back from intervention in Hungary, from tearing down the Berlin wall, from toppling Castro. The Russians have held back in Vietnam, retreated in the Cuban missile crisis, and tolerated peacemaking efforts in South Asia, where once they might have sought profit in stirring things up.

By sacrificing power within their alliances and by practicing a self-imposed restraint, the big powers have enhanced their ability to keep the peace but lost some of their capacity to build more peace, to reach a great European settlement, as they might have shortly after World World II, or to extricate themselves from unwanted conflict, say, in Southeast Asia.

I

I have taken this long detour to sketch some background and and to set up some standards by which I think we ought always to discuss change in the world. Change is a function not only of the accidents of history or geography or personality, infinite though these are in variety, but also of slowly evolving conditions in the modern world, such as the nature of modern weapons. We talk much today, as we have since World War II, about atomic deterrence, arms control, nuclear strategy, and so on. Our unfortunate lack of progress in controlling the means of war has made much of this debate sound unchanging, and thus we forget the great and changing diplomatic significance of the mechanical facts of life — the superfluous nature of bases in Turkey, as we discovered at the time of the missile crisis, and similar psychological changes that our technical posture induces in us and in others.

There are many other such facts of life that determine change: the economic power balances in the world, the resignation of Europe from most activity in the non-European world, the coming to power everywhere of new generations to whom the postwar conflicts and ambitions have intellectual rather than emotional significance, and so on.

We cannot think about flux in the Communist world unless we are mindful of this world-wide flux and its constancy.

I was reminded recently that Schopenhauer once called us journalists the second hand on the clock of history. He was slandering us, of course, because he meant that we record the most minute changes, tend to give equal significance to each, occupy a new position every instant, and never worry about being really right. With considerable malice, he observed that second hands on clocks are almost always made of a much less valuable and much more perishable alloy than the hands that record the minutes and the hours. (I assume that diplomats and officials are the minute-men and that academicians or scholars are the plodding recorders of the hours of history.)

But I find this a very valuable metaphor because it reinforces my own assumption about all three hands on the face of this clock. We are merely the external indicators of a constant ticking away and movement inside. In lecture series and books we deal with change in an artificial language; it is 4 o'clock, a time of Stalin, or 8:30, the time of Mao; it is dark or light, good or bad. It is important, however, that whenever we glance at the clock to see what has changed, we remember that change is never-ending and gradual.

The year 1948, for instance, brought us almost simultaneously the Communist seizure of Czechoslovakia and the defection or expulsion from the Soviet bloc of Tito's Yugoslavia. The confluence of these two events alone makes it impossible to say whether 1948 marked the final triumph of Soviet expansionism in Eastern Europe or the beginning of the disintegration of the Stalinist bid for empire. Obviously, it was both, though our perception does not always grasp the trend of things in time.

Finally, in discussing change somewhere else, let us always remember the change in ourselves, and remember to calculate the interaction of these changes. In that same year of 1948, for instance, the West finally came to recognize the grim challenge of the events in Czechoslovakia and the great opportunity of the events in Yugoslavia. The emphasis then was upon military and political combat to save the rest of Europe, but simultaneously we began an offensive effort to encourage disintegration in Communist Europe, even if we did not yet fully appreciate our opportunities or the fact that East-West agreement of a certain type would ultimately be a safer and sometimes better weapon in the East-West conflict.

Because change in the Communist world and change in ours always go together and the one always influences the other in ways that it is almost impossible to predict or even analyze, modesty and open-mindedness in policy and analysis are absolutely essential if the truth be served. Whenever we glance at the clock to see what time it is in the Communist world, we must remember that they are glancing at us and that to a certain extent we are each setting our clock by the other's. And this periodic adjustment of the clock on one side or the other may be as much a function of our own perception as of the real movement that occurs.

If I were writing this in Moscow, I could be giving a most convincing argument about flux in the Western world. Writing in Moscow, I would find Americans, in particular, to be profoundly "revisionist" in their attitudes toward the Soviet Union, no longer waging the cold war against Russians in the spirit in which they once waged it, and learning to live side by side at least with some Communist societies, rather than hoping for their overthrow or collapse. And as a Communist or even just as a good Russian, I would probably attribute this change in

America to the effective policies of deterrence that my government has practiced against the United States these past two decades, forcing the Americans to outgrow the vanity of their "unconditional" victory in World War II and the psychopathic fear of communism and the disease of McCarthyism at home. I would say that America is still, in some vestigial sense, a nation with imperial ambitions, or at least with a sense of imperial mission in the world, as demonstrated in Vietnam or the Dominican Republic. I would say that she had to be resisted in these places, but not in hot-headed fashion, for she shares our own desire for peace. And I would find great encouragement in the fact of continuing flux in the West, in the fact that the American empire is beginning to break up, that its hegemony in Europe is being slowly worn down not only by Gaullism but by the strong desire of her former satellites to develop their own forms of national life and expression. By just changing a few names, I could say there many of the same things I would say here.

Quite apart from the familiar Communist celebrations of the collapse of colonialism and the progress of various types of socialism, I could find in Moscow pragmatic justification for the broad lines of Soviet policy, and I would counsel continuing adjustments of policy to the present time of competition and restraint and the avoidance of direct conflict. And I would hold out the hope of moving toward effective collaboration or cooperation between the Communist and Western worlds in the future, even in the midst of continued efforts to get the best of the Americans in every situation that develops.

In Moscow I would claim credit for having brought about these changes in the camp of the enemy, just as we here claim credit for many of the changes and adjustments in the Communist world. If I could somehow stand between the two worlds, a more objective appraisal might be possible — but again, the very fact that we each are working upon the state of mind of the other becomes itself a fact of the relationship.

What I have tried to describe is not just a crude symmetry, wherein one side seems to be the mirror image of the other, but rather a dynamic relationship such as that which results from two mirrors which face each other and infinitely reflect the reflection of the other.

II

Flux in the Communist world is so great that we could devote all this space and more to discuss just the Moscow-Peking conflict, or the internal dynamics of the Soviet Union, or the psychology of East Germans, or economic agitation in Czechoslovakia, or the splintered Communist movement of Japan, or the great power of the Communists in Indonesia that has now brought them to a great — and for us hopeful — catastrophe. Our agony in Vietnam alone, agony in analyzing the situation as well as in dealing with it, demonstrates my point. We are struggling with "Communists" in the jungle, the Viet Cong, and the "Communist" government in North Vietnam, and with the ideological as well as practical, the tactical as well as strategic, relevance to the war of the "Communist" government of China and the "Communist" government of the Soviet Union. To talk of "Communists" in this situation, then, is to say virtually nothing; it may still describe a certain emotional orientation, but the practical significance of that orientation requires elaborate embellishment.

So too, in "Communist" Europe. To speak of a "Communist," or even of a Polish or Hungarian Communist, tells you very little about him. The great insight of hindsight now tells us that it may never have meant very much; that the local and historical and psychological setting of each of the societies that fell under Communist control has always exerted a powerful and perhaps even dominant influence over the nature of communism in each place. But the interaction of change in the Soviet Union and elsewhere in the Communist world with the larger changes in the world and in our own attitudes has surely demonstrated that the differences *inside* Communist nations and parties and the differences *among* them are at least as important to the politics of the world today as the differences between Communists and non-Communists.

To help us tell the time on the clock and analyze the situation, let me revert to my journalistic habits and take some of the headlines of the present time and of recent years to make a list of what I believe to have been the six major changes in the Communist world.

Perhaps the most profound change, which I have already touched on in another context, is demonstrated by having me discuss change in the Communist world just as the 23rd Congress of the Soviet Communist Party convened in Moscow.

In another day, no one in his right mind would have accepted this assignment without knowing the consequences of this supreme, or once supreme, assembly of Soviet politicians. These congresses are, and to some extent remain, major events to those who either practice or study communism, because they ratify, record, and initiate major turns and sometimes even doctrines of Soviet policy at home and abroad.

That I accept this assignment without knowing the outcome of the Congress is evidence of what I call change number one: the flux in the Communist world is *so* great that not even a Soviet Party congress or decree or individual is likely to alter our analysis of basic trends. And we can have confidence in much of that analysis because the flux itself has brought us a flood of valuable information and insight. Out of conflict comes not only news, but truth.

What happened at the Moscow congress — and what in any week the leaders of the Soviet Union may wish to decide — is not any longer the certain or even likely inspiration of political change in the Communist world. This is truly an extraordinary fact of evolution, made all the more important by Moscow's recognition of it and acquiescence in it. It has no choice. It must negotiate and manipulate where once it decreed.

Change number two on my list, which I have also mentioned in passing, comes not from a headline but from the lack of it. Every now and then (this very moment, for all I know), American planes zoom in fast and low over North Vietnam and attack an antiaircraft missile installation of Soviet design and manufacture. Some of the missiles are fired and find their mark, shooting down American fliers and killing some of them.

Some of the American bombs also find their mark, destroying the missile sites and killing some of their crews, including Russians. The remarkable thing about these exchanges is that very few Americans and Russians know that a few Americans and a few Russians are actually dying these days in combat against each other — their first official combat, in fact, in modern history.

Despite this war and because of it, Moscow and Washington are engaged in a conspiracy of silence about the conflict between them, because they do not want it to grow or to involve their prestige in direct confrontation. The best way to avoid a battle is to pretend to ignore it, at least when you are so powerful that the very acknowledgment of conflict requires a response.

This conspiracy, of course, is only a part of their larger collaboration to avoid war. What is so significant about Vietnam is that we are demonstrating in blood our desire to have this collaboration survive the strains of rival commitments and obligations, tactical interests, and ideological pretensions. We are living an extraordinarily sophisticated double life that balances self-interest with a profound and sympathetic understanding of the self-interest of the other side. And if you are not as surprised as I am that American policy has become capable of such sophistication, you do, I trust, share with me an awareness of the shock that such a double life and love-hate partnership imply for Soviet politics, whose whole system was built upon enmity to our own and dedicated to its overthrow.

The debate that this change produced inside the Soviet Union and between Moscow and Peking is much more than a doctrinal dispute as to whether war is or is not inevitable between the Communist and so-called capitalist systems. The issue in debate is whether Communists dare place national self-interest and survival — and therefore cooperation or collaboration, or at least reduction of conflict with us — ahead of their philosophical and emotional investment in world-wide revolution. And while a revolution deferred is not necessarily a revolution canceled, I tend to agree with the orthodox Communists who remain in Moscow and the dogmatic ones in Peking. They are right to argue that by its self-serving policies through most of its history and especially in the past decade, the Soviet Union has helped to make communism as a doctrine increasingly irrelevant to some of the most important developments in international affairs.

Change number three takes me back to a news story that came in on the wires last February from Naples, Italy. It said, "The Naples archdiocese today forbade Roman Catholics to help a campaign for a monument to Pope John XXIII. The reason: the Italian Communist Party is running the campaign."

I do not know where to begin the catalogue of changes implied by that little two-sentence dispatch. It denotes the recovery and relative stability of Italy (as of all Western Europe), due in large measure to the "anti-Communist" policies of the United States since World War II. These policies, in turn, produced a situation in which the once-menacing Communist Party of Italy was forced to compete for power in an open and democratic way, where once it dreamed of seizing power by coup. And this, of course, led to the split of the Left in Italy, luring the Socialists into government and responsibility because they preferred power to dogma. The situation has raised demands among Italian Communists for a more local brand of communism, free of the alien, restraining, and increasingly irrelevant doctrines of the Soviet Union. That, in turn, has proved to be another major blow against the Soviet hold on the world Communist movement and has had the backlash effect of inspiring the Italian Communists to keep searching for a more indigenous political purpose. That search is pursued even when it requires open criticism of the Soviet Union, as after the recent trials of two Soviet writers.

In short, the Italian Communists have moved in a decade through what they called "polycentrism" and other justifications of local opportunism, to their present pass: robbed by

Catholics, no less, of the chance to erect a simple monument to a pope. Not only are the Italian Communists criticizing Moscow and refusing Soviet orders and demanding for themselves what is now called "internal Party democracy," but they are competing with the Church for the affections of the faithful and being denied entry to the Church. How demeaning!

The pattern of local adjustment by Communists is different in detail but not in kind in France and India and Brazil and throughout the non-Communist world. It has evoked a traumatic readjustment that causes infinite dispute and division. Most of that division is tactical, but it has robbed communism of its doctrinal appeal, which always rested on its great tactical strength and international cohesion. To study communism nowadays anywhere, you must look deep into the political fabric of individual societies and you must read papal encyclicals with at least as much attention as *Pravda* editorials.

Change number four on my list is a comparable development *inside* the Communist world, thus making it of even greater political significance.

Name a Communist country and we could speak for hours about its altered relationship with the Soviet Union, with its own people, with other Communist nations, and with its undeniable ambitions for dealings with other, non-Communist nations. Tito's Yugoslavia was for too long unique and sensational to be the proper example here, though it has had an enormous psychological impact upon other Communist governments. Albania, Czechoslovakia, Hungary, Poland, Bulgaria, East Germany, North Korea, North Vietnam — each tells its own story.

In recent years perhaps the best example of the extent of change is that of Romania. It borders directly upon the Soviet Union, has no direct access to the West (unless you count Yugoslavia, as you might), and has not confused the process of international change with so-called liberalization or democratization or de-Stalinization at home. It is a good example also because it has summarized its policy in a formal declaration of independence that is almost as ringing as our own.

The declaration was issued two years ago and had to be swallowed whole by both the Khrushchev regime and its successor. It stated: "There are not and cannot be any 'no-alternative' patterns and recipes [in the Communist world] . . . no one can decide what is and what is not correct for other countries and parties." There cannot be a "parent" party and a "son" party, it declared; none is "superior" and none "subordinate" and none has a "privileged position or can impose its line and opinions on other parties."

As I said, this was only the most forthright declaration. The other Communist governments have all maneuvered and rebelled, now here, now there, with or without declarations, with or without reservations, and there is no point in wondering here which was the most important or, to Moscow, the most detrimental.

The moves toward independence developed in an international setting that forced Nikita Khrushchev, like Winston Churchill, to try to substitute the notion of "commonwealth" for that of empire; but Moscow, like London, failed to give the new concept much meaning or dynamic value. Even the barest forms of economic collaboration in Eastern Europe are now subject to the normal stresses and impediments that national sovereignty imposes anywhere.

I am not suggesting that most of the Communist nations of Europe are not dependent upon the Soviet Union, economically and politically, nor that rebelliousness has come over them at the same rate. I am saying that there is a fundamental change in what it *means* to be a Communist government, and one of the things it means now is the *right*, as in any other government, to make your own calculation of dependency and independence and to maneuver within the limits of domestic strength and capacity to serve an indigenous concept of the national interest.

The clever and novel aspect of the Romanian rebellion was the way in which it exploited the fifth great change in the Communist world — a rebellion or defection so great that it must rank as a wholly separate development. This is, of course, the defection of Communist China, which established Peking as not only a separate but also a rival center of Communist doctrine, tactics, and strategy. I emphasize tactics and strategy because we are still too much the slaves of caution in calling the Moscow-Peking dispute an "ideological" conflict. Probably from the start, and certainly for many years now, I believe, this dispute has been the expression of a conflict of vital national interests and as such has been waged in a spirit of national, and not just ideological, competition.

Each of these great Communist societies is using all the means at its disposal, economic and military as well as diplomatic and propagandistic, to promote its own interests and positively to injure those of the other. The story of their contest is too familiar to need much retelling — the Soviet cut-off of nuclear and finally economic aid; the diminishing pattern of trade; the conflict over India; the radically different approaches to us in the United States; the fierce competition for the support of other Communist parties and governments; the equally energetic rivalry and hostility in the search for influence in the non-Communist world; the accusations of meddling in their respective internal affairs; the shadowboxing along their immense frontier; the virtual enjoyment on the part of one over difficulty and disaster besetting the other, as in China's response to the Soviet retreat from Cuba and the Soviet response to Chinese failure in Algeria.

I would now rank the cold war between China and Russia with our own against Russia, and I believe that it will last much longer because it arises from direct conflict in many areas of vital concern to both, while our own cold war resulted much more from indirect conflicts of interest.

It is not just because they are both Communist nations that China and Russia are so deeply engaged in this battle. It is also because they are neighbors. It is because of their tangled history. It is because they are of different races. It is a feud fed by the many injuries inflicted in the conduct of the feud.

Not only have both governments now acknowledged and resigned themselves to the low state of their relations, but they have planned in their policies for the continuation of the conflict, so that the grievances will be compounded — quarterly.

Whereas the cold war between East and West could be diminished by a gradual strategic balance of power, the cold war between Moscow and Peking is being perpetuated by the disparities, jealousies, and resentments born of economic and military imbalance. And it is being perpetuated by the cynical responses of the other Communist governments, most of whom seem to wish to prevent a final rupture, which might replace a single orthodoxy of the past by two new ones, while also preventing a rapprochement that would inhibit their own freedom of maneuver.

It does not so much matter, I think, whether the Russians have 65 or 75 of the world's Communist parties on their side, as against a dozen or two that side with the Chinese. What matters is that each of the world's Communist parties, like each of the smaller Communist governments, now wishes to preserve a choice of alignment and a freedom of maneuver, not only between the two giants but beyond them.

So deep is this feud that it must have a profound effect also upon the domestic policies of all the Communist nations, and particularly those of the two main contenders. "China policy" is a major issue in the Kremlin and "Kremlin policy" is perhaps an even greater issue in Peking. This, too, is debilitating, as we can judge from the effects of the much less serious domestic divisions we have experienced in our country about how to deal with real or presumed enemies.

That brings me to a final and basic change, number six on my list of fluxes — the profound change in the domestic life and social and economic politics of the Soviet Union. It was exactly ten years ago, at another Soviet Party congress, that Khrushchev rose to denounce Stalin as a psychopath who had done to his system everything its enemies had always said he had done. Stalin was accused not only of butchering loyal Communist comrades by the thousands, but also of almost proving that the Communist system was incapable of surviving the tyranny that the system itself had preached and imposed upon the Russian people.

I cannot decide whether the more remarkable thing about politics in Russia ever since has been the fitful destruction of what is known as Stalinism or the psychological effect of the turn against Stalinism as such. Surely Khrushchev's purpose was to save Communist power, not to bury it, but he came close to an awareness and acknowledgment that it could not survive, and certainly never prosper, unless it purged itself of its own essential nature. If the orthodoxy had merely been corrupted by Stalin, as Khrushchev at first tried to maintain, it could have been healed. But the effect of Soviet politics in the past decade has been to redefine the orthodoxy, which really has meant destroying it.

With or without Stalin, China and Poland and Romania might have rebelled sooner or later. With or without Stalinism, the economic systems of the Communist world might have been reformed or redesigned, in a single way or in the many different ways that we now see.

The overriding significance of de-Stalinization as practiced for over ten years is the move throughout Soviet society to create institutional guarantees against the worst features of Stalin's communism. And this, I believe, will gradually give us a very different order of Soviet communism. The monopoly of power that Communists always demanded is not only being broken; it is in some instances being willingly surrendered to stimulate popularity, or economic progress, or a more effective system of checks and balances that will guard against abuses of power.

All this is the cause of great anxiety among the Soviet leaders and people, and it is not a trend without detours or obstacles. But it is a profound social evolution whose outcome neither we nor the Russians themselves can yet predict.

III

Having listed what seem to me the major changes occurring in the Communist world, let me deal briefly with some of their consequences. This exercise gets almost too complicated unless we agree to oversimplify and deal in one dimension at a time. For each of the changes I have listed interacts with the others: de-Stalinization has affected the Chinese defection; the Chinese defection has infected the rebellions against Moscow throughout the Communist world, and these rebellions have altered the very nature of the Communist parties and governments. In turn, the splintering of the Soviet world and the weakening of Communist orthodoxy, if not ideology, has been a most important element in the changing relationship between the Soviet Union and the United States. And all of these developments have combined to inhibit the power of the Soviet Union and of communism in general.

Taking these changes one at a time, I would list the following consequences as among the most important:

Since Stalin, the Soviet political system has moved unquestionably away from one-man dictatorship to an increasingly bureaucratized and institutional form. The Soviet leadership has had to recognize and accept, and at times even welcome, the limits on its own power. Together these trends have pointed toward a much more conventional, though certainly not Western, political structure based on a complicated pattern of popular motivation and institutional negotiation.

I know from my experience in Washington, as well as in Moscow, that to share power institutionally is a more humiliating requirement for political leaders than to share it simply with other leaders. Power that is traded away, even for profit, in an institutional manner, is not easily reclaimed or recovered.

There has been much confusion of this trend in Soviet politics with the parallel but far less consistent trend toward what is called liberalization and relaxation of governmental restraints upon the population and arbitrariness in dealing with individual citizens. The two trends are obviously related, but they are not synonymous.

You can have institutional power-sharing among institutions that remain reactionary — in fact, they almost always are at least conservative in their habits. And you can decree liberalization under one-man dictatorship; it can be benign.

The important and I think promising thing in the Soviet Union is that the two trends are developing together. Liberalization, therefore, whether introduced from above or wrested from below, is more likely to survive when it is reinforced in institutional habits, legal systems, and a system, no matter how crude, of checks and balances.

I do not think that we can anticipate the speed of Soviet liberalization, either in political or economic thought and life. There are strong forces of resistance, especially in the Communist Party, whose very legitimacy depends upon a concept of political supremacy and arbitrariness. But I think we can expect other Soviet institutions and groups to maintain considerable pressure for more and more relaxation of this arbitrary power, if only because they wish in this way to rally popular support for their own power.

The consequences of change in the Soviet bloc of Eastern Europe are even more difficult to comprehend because the picture at the moment, and in the foreseeable future, is so different from country to country.

Each, as I said, now has much greater room for maneuver, but the exploitation of that new power is determined not only by the over-all situation but by the specific economic capacities of each Communist society, the supply of population, the skill and security of the leadership, and the heritage of national institutions and aspirations.

It is fair, however, to generalize that each feels itself less dependent upon the Soviet Union as fear of the military or economic power of the West recedes. Moreover, the Communist leaders of Eastern Europe all seem to have learned to some degree that they can no longer rely upon Soviet military or even economic power if they mismanage their own affairs. Thus, they are appeasing or appealing to their own people, some because they have to and others because they want to. If the Soviet Union hesitated, even ten years ago, before intervening militarily in Hungary, how much less certain the Communist rulers of Eastern Europe must be of this and lesser forms of help today.

Within the pattern of change in East Europe, it is fair to check the clock by the standard of domestic de-Stalinization, or general improvement of life, and of international desatellization, or independence from Moscow. Here again are two trends which, though mutually reinforcing, do not by any means go hand in hand. Poland and Hungary are dependent upon economic ties to the Soviet Union that may for a long time affect their international freedom of action; yet they have, at different times, made great strides in evolving new patterns of domestic rule. Romania and Albania rebelled against Moscow first, and it is far from clear what their domestic development will be.

But domestic popularity or strength reduces dependence upon Moscow, while rebellion against Moscow requires strength. So we can expect a dynamic interaction.

In assessing domestic change in Eastern Europe, I would make one other generalization: it seems to be moving from literary and political ferment toward agitation in economics and in the awakening of a new nationalism. The only safe prediction about Eastern Europe is that its Communist governments will, now in concert, now in competition, function more and more as expressions of a national, if not always popular, interest, and that they will therefore seek ever more freedom of action between East and West.

In a different sense, this will be true also of the Communist governments of Asia, which are even nearer to the conflict between Moscow and Peking. The Mongolians, Koreans, and Vietnamese will look to the Communist world for support because that is, willy-nilly, the only place they can now find it, but they undoubtedly will try to exploit the Peking-Moscow competition for maximum national profit.

As I have already noted, the consequence of the "localization" of Communist movements in non-Communist nations has caused confusion and frustration, a conflict between a deeply emotional international loyalty to the movement, or even yet to Moscow, and political opportunity at home. As a result, the Communist parties of India and Japan, several in Latin America and in the Middle East, have formally or virtually been torn apart by tactical disputes, some of which then take the shape of alignment with Moscow or Peking.

The overriding result is a weakening of Communist efforts everywhere and a confidence of non-Communist governments in handling them, not to mention the growth of American confidence in not daily dreading them. Both Moscow and Peking, I believe, retain an emotional bond and sense of debt to their Communist clients abroad, but there is even less reason now than in the past to expect either to respond automatically to the needs of these available but not always welcome local agents.

As the Russians discovered in Cuba and Africa, and the Chinese in Indonesia and many other places, loyalty to Communists implies certain dangerous or at least costly commitments that no government likes to assume blindly. And if there are suspicion and doubt about the degree of support flowing in each direction between the local Communist movements and the centers of Communist power, we can expect more and more disintegration, until the time comes, if it has not already come, when we must ask what it really means to speak of a "Communist world."

The major consequence of the Soviet-Chinese conflict is to accelerate this trend of disintegration, and, as I suggested, I expect the conflict to feed on itself. We have already reached the point where grievances must not only be forgotten or overcome, but undone and compensated for if there is to be a new era of Soviet-Chinese cooperation. And I do not now foresee the time when Moscow will be willing to take great risks on China's behalf, or vice versa. A healing of their rift is not likely unless the threat to both from outside becomes incomparably greater than is now likely and greater than the threat or danger that each now poses for the other.

On the contrary, I expect the rivalry and competition to pile insult upon injury, over Vietnam and Asia generally, over atomic weapons and nuclear age strategy, over détente with the West, over influence in Algeria or Ghana or Egypt or Brazil, over diplomatic and economic rivalries in India and Pakistan.

IV

The United States will play a pivotal role in this conflict, for we are the third corner or leg of the triangular battle for spheres of influence in the world today.

U.S. policy makers will no longer be able to rest with calculations of this or that "Communist" threat, for from now on we shall always have to consider, first, which Communists, and we shall find ourselves increasingly trying to enlist one of the Communist powers on our side against the other.

The imperfect collusion of Moscow and Washington on behalf of India against China and, more recently, for peace between India and Pakistan over Kashmir was only a foretaste of these exercises in triangularism. Nor do I foreclose the same thing happening along the other sides, occasionally Moscow and Peking against us, and Peking and Washington against Moscow.

We have not often put it this way, but the United States and Communist China have been partners of a sort for a decade in encouraging independent and essentially anti-Soviet conduct in the Communist nations of Eastern Europe. And there may come a time when we can more openly recognize and acknowledge other coincidences of interest. The West Germans, for instance, already speak seriously, if somewhat prematurely, of encouraging Communist China so that the Soviet Union will have more and more trouble in its rear and feel compelled to seek a more durable settlement in Central Europe.

We are witnessing not just the expansion of a bipolar contest into a triangular one. The complexity of this three-way confusion is multiplied many times when you add the predictable effort of other, weaker nations to join this free-for-all of changing and undulating alignments.

I have returned now to where I began: the interacting nature of change itself. For the consequence of all this, and perhaps the cause of much of it, namely, the great change inside the Soviet Union, has been the dissipation of fear and rigidity and therefore discipline in the West. The evolution of an independent nationalism among the Communist nations and the loss of strength in the Communist movement in general have eroded our own alliance systems, robbed them of the glue of anti-communism and emboldened less powerful governments, not only France, to hold and express and act upon views and policies different from our own.

And all of this is imposing profound changes upon us, the mere listing of which raises another complicated topic. The preoccupation with China, though the Soviet Union remains the only power that can injure us directly at the moment; the agony of Vietnam; the relative neglect of Europe — all these are emerging as a part of our response to change in the Communist world. The confusion has also diminished our zeal for foreign aid. It has made our responses to instability and crisis elsewhere much more pragmatic. We wish we could dismantle some of the military alliances of another decade, finding them irritants and divisive as often as we have found them useful, and we are building a complicated pattern of new relations with every nation, whether nominally ally or neutral between communism and its opposite. We tolerate a nation that calls itself Communist right on our doorstep; we occupy another to prevent it from going Communist. We no longer write off a nation as "lost" to communism, even if it chooses undemocratic political or unpalatable economic forms.

The very strange pattern of collusion and conflict between the Soviet Union and the United States has taught us all a measure of humility in presuming either friendship or enmity to be permanent. We have come to regard the Soviet people as real and human, with identifiable interests, and they have come to regard us in the same way. We not only cooperate and compete, we also seek safety in a delicate balance of arms and arms control; we have learned not to be dogmatic about any feature of our relationship.

And because we celebrate the obvious diminution of Soviet

power, we have become much more easily accustomed to the obvious diminution of our own, which makes for fewer "victories" in foreign affairs, but also for fewer ulcers in our domestic politics.

V

Finally, the flux in the Communist world has yielded a result that I am afraid is not yet widely recognized. Perhaps it is important only to someone who has had to live in a Communist society and to suffer its insufferable ideology and propaganda.

The most seductive element of that ideology has always been its sense of certainty and confidence and its claim to be the "last stage" in the political development of man and society. That claim placed communism above capitalism and certainly above feudalism in the Communist textbook. It encouraged young people around the world to look upon communism as a "higher form" of political organization and the wave of the future. To be a Communist meant to be advanced, to be ahead of your time, to be working for your children and grandchildren, and thus to be an agent of the gods themselves.

We now have our answer to that awful question which we used to address to the Communists but which neither they nor we could answer: what, unless you expect the world to stand still, will come after communism? My Russian friends used to reply: a higher form of communism. But that, clearly, was nonsense. The answer, plainly, is *many communisms*, just as there are many capitalisms and nationalisms. And this diversity robs the ideology of its greatest single asset: the aspect of uniqueness and religious certainty.

Those of us who have engaged Communists in philosophical rather than political debate have also been searching for a demonstration of what we have regarded as the fundamental flaw in the Communist theory. Real communism, the perfect sharing and perfect working of the system, it was clear, depended at all times upon a basic change in the nature of man.

Much of the blood that has been shed in our time in the name of this ideology was shed because men would not conform to its precepts, would not behave as it said they must behave for this world to be perfect, would not be selfless and subservient to society and ready to lose themselves in the collective mass and in the collective's notion of the common good. The blood was spilled either to make men conform or to eliminate them so that others might. It was shed in the confidence that a future generation would indeed have a different "human nature."

What is encouraging and even satisfying in the Western liberal, pragmatic, and relativistic sense is that communism has failed to change the nature of man as it said it could or would. It is now man who is changing communism and making it conform to his own imperfect and possibly damned but quite traditional nature.

This development alone would justify our treating Communist nations and Communists not as a messianic challenge but as a normal, if troublesome, political and military challenge. Real men and real nations and real politics lie behind the façade of the Communist ideology and deserve to be treated as such by the real nations and real men that live behind *our* ideological façade.

The Soviet Union will be fifty years old next year. Only in the last of these five decades has she enjoyed anything like a feeling of security. Politically, this means that for forty of her years her leaders were struggling not only against weakness but for survival itself in what they took to be a hostile environment.

They have now finally overcome starvation and civil strife and established a viable if struggling industrial machine. They have made themselves militarily as secure as anyone can be and they have achieved enough political stability to be capable of bloodless, if not yet orderly, transfers of power.

It is only now that we in the West can see this change for what it is really worth, though it has been in the making all along. We see a Russian personality behind the Soviet inscrutability. We see annoying secrecy where once we saw only baffling mystery. But we also see real political conflict and real human aspiration. We are, or should be, big enough and secure enough and wise enough to draw the proper policy lessons from our recognition of this change.

Our recognition of this change, of the profound flux in the Communist world, may be even more important to the nature of world politics than the change itself.

SOVIET FOREIGN POLICY SINCE KHRUSHCHEV

PHILIP E. MOSELY

Khrushchev's successors have continued the low-key posture which the Kremlin adopted after the traumatic experience of the Cuban missile crisis, in October 1962. Indeed, the Brezhnev-Kosygin team has been more consistent than its sometimes volatile and usually voluble predecessor in muting the challenge of Soviet long-range ambitions and avoiding any new confrontation with the great power and influence of the United States. By a policy of restraint in words as well as deeds, Brezhnev and Kosygin have reaped intangible but important gains for Soviet prestige. By choosing a posture of unaggressive patience, the new leadership has created rather quickly the image of a "responsible" and cautious Soviet Union which can be a desirable political partner in the interplay of world politics.

Under Brezhnev's and Kosygin's direction the Soviet government has wiped away the fears of a renewal of Soviet nuclear adventurism. It was perhaps to be expected that the dangerous crisis of October 1962 would leave a deeper and more lasting imprint on American than on European policy thinking. Be that as it may, influential leaders and opinion-formers in Western Europe are much more inclined today than most Americans to believe that the Soviet leadership is now committed in perpetuity to a low-risk policy. This divergence in perspective is one of the main sources of disarray within the Atlantic Alliance.

Whatever other NATO governments may say publicly, President Charles de Gaulle is not alone in believing that NATO has now become dispensable simply because the Soviet challenge to the security of the West has vanished. For almost fifty years, ever since the Russian Revolution of 1917, the rest of the world has been waiting and hoping for the time when, no longer bent on fomenting world revolution, the Soviet regime would abandon its messianic arrogance and would begin to behave as one great power among others. According to de Gaulle and many other Europeans, that golden age has now arrived and nothing serious will henceforth disturb the new and welcome atmosphere of peace and trust.

I

Among conflicting explanations of the new and cautious posture of Soviet policy, two major schools of thought stand out. One school holds, in brief, that the present posture of caution has been forced upon the Kremlin by unforeseen and unfavorable shifts in the world balance of power. Contrary to Stalin's and Khrushchev's expectations, the acquisition of great nuclear power has not enhanced the ability of the Soviet Union to achieve its goals or to extend its writ beyond the existing boundaries of the Communist grouping of states. The Kremlin, like the Pentagon earlier, was reluctant to acknowledge the limitations of nuclear force. Between the Suez crisis of 1956 and the Cuban missile crisis of 1962 Khrushchev sought repeatedly for political gains commensurate with this vast and costly addition to the Soviet military arsenal. Indeed, the decision to place

Soviet missiles in Cuba was basically a reflex of Khrushchev's exasperation at his inability to leap beyond the emerging nuclear stalemate and achieve decisive political gains.

Even before this rebuff to Soviet expansionism, the Kremlin's hopes had suffered many grave disappointments in the years since World War II. Contrary to Roosevelt's fears and Stalin's hopes, America had not withdrawn after the war to a position of self-isolation and passivity. Instead, it responded to a series of Soviet and Chinese Communist challenges by becoming the most powerful nation in the world. Nor did the American economy undergo the widely predicted postwar depression, on the 1929–1933 pattern, which was supposed to undermine American strength and destroy the prestige of the free-enterprise system. Western, non-Communist Europe was restored to economic health with remarkable speed and has gone on to new achievements which in turn exert a strong pull on the forcibly Communized countries of East Central Europe. The dismantling of the long-established colonial empires has been followed by much confusion, disorder, and uncertainty. However, except in Cuba, which presented a special situation, this great process of change has not led to any outright victories for Communist policy. Finally, the one great postwar success of communism — in mainland China — has been followed by a profound split between the two greatest Communist powers and by a bitter struggle between them.

According to this first school, the present Soviet policy of caution is due in part to the strong posture of the United States and the support of its friends, and in part to numerous unforeseen obstacles that have frustrated the expansion of Soviet power and influence. Therefore, if American power and leadership can be weakened, if some of the obstacles can be surmounted, or if new opportunities for political gains are offered to Soviet policy, the world can, in this view, expect the Kremlin to renew, almost overnight, its efforts to achieve new political or military conquests consonant with a more favorable estimate of potential gains and risks. According to this prognosis, the West and its friends, and even neutrals, would be very unwise, just at a time when twenty years of sacrifices and risks have begun to pay off, to abandon those very instruments of strength and cohesion that have brought about at long last this state of relative balance and stability.

Another school of thought, defined oversimply, holds, on the contrary, that the post-1962 moderating of Soviet ambitions and methods has been due primarily to basic changes within the Soviet system itself and hardly at all to the success of "containment" exerted from without. Supporters of this view point, and rightly so, to many significant changes of mood within Soviet society. Beginning with Khrushchev's still unpublished de-Stalinization speech of February 1956, and proceeding in fits and starts, many aspects of Soviet life have been opened up to reappraisal in a way that would make Stalin turn over in his grave.

No doubt Khrushchev believed that his decision to authorize the publication of *One Day in the Life of Ivan Denisovich*, by Alexander Solzhenitsyn, would reinforce the Kremlin's "new look" in a purely beneficial way. A frank admission of the reality and the cruelty of Stalin's forced-labor camps would redound vastly to Khrushchev's credit and enlist widespread support for his renovation of the Soviet system. The acknowledgment of past massive injustice would poultice the deep wounds of Soviet society and would throw up a moral dike against any possible new wave of wholesale and undiscriminating terror. It would etch sharply the contrast between the Stalinist and the Khrushchevian styles of rule.

De-Stalinization accomplished this and much else. But it had other and undesired effects. The deep-rooted skepticism of many Soviet people toward the official "line" was now justified in their eyes by weighty evidence offered from on high. If Stalin was no longer "the all-wise teacher" and "leader of the world proletariat" but a torturer and a bungler; if the concentration camps, which had formerly been declared a concoction of anti-Soviet slander, were now exposed to the light of day, just what could Soviet people believe from now on? Were there not other past or present "official truths" which might someday dissolve into their opposite? And perhaps other nations and their leaders were right in rejecting and combating the Soviet recipe for their salvation, Communist-style.

Khrushchev's shaking up of the Soviet "petrified forest" was indispensable and long overdue. Yet, while releasing important efforts to improve the system, this process has also stimulated numerous symptoms of a retreat from ideology. Today Soviet people respond actively to concrete and tangible ameliorations in their way of life, rather than to lofty and messianic goals. Postrevolutionary spiritual fatigue, which was both delayed and compounded by Russia's titanic exertions and sacrifices in World War II, has invaded large segments of Soviet society, much to the discomfiture of the leadership.

One minor but telling measure of this changed mood is reflected in the resurgence of political jokes. The sardonic humor of the ordinary Soviet citizen, long inhibited by Stalinist terror, has been rising to the surface again. When the poor harvest of 1963, compounded by the backward state of much of Soviet agriculture, led the government to make large-scale purchases of wheat in Canada and the United States, a question-and-answer joke quickly made the rounds. Question: "What proof is there that the Soviet Union has the greatest farm expert in the world?" Answer: "Because he sows grain in Kazakhstan and it comes up in Saskatchewan." Khrushchev's feelings were hurt by this sally, and he launched a solemn countercampaign to explain that, whereas Stalin would have made the people go without bread, he, in contrast, had spent scarce foreign currency and gold to assure an adequate food supply for his people.

The numerous demonstrations of Soviet inadequacies — in agriculture, in the poor quality and high prices of consumer goods, in the recent slowdown in the rate of growth — do not add up to a political challenge to the basic strength of the regime. They have led rather to a kind of escapism, a retreat into apathy and skepticism. Rather than let themselves be taken in again by the familiar summons to revolutionary romanticism, many Soviet people have adopted a kind of "show-me-first" attitude, seeking small but personal enjoyments rather than pursuing vast collective goals.

This same atmosphere influences, but does not determine, the spirit in which many Soviet people think about the role of their country in world politics. Since the Soviet system has imposed many cruelties and prolonged hardships on its own people, perhaps it is not worth recommending so ardently to all people, everywhere. If Soviet agriculture is still hobbling after almost fifty years, then just possibly Communist propaganda should be more modest than was Khrushchev in recommending the collective-farm system to the highly efficient farmers of Denmark or Sweden as well as to the poor peasants of India or Ghana. Soviet people have greeted with relief the repeated assurances by Khrushchev and his successors that "revolution is not an export commodity" and that "each nation must make its own revolution" by its own forces. They are deeply pleased when, in sharp contradiction to Peking's infatuation with "continuous revolution," the Soviet leaders emphasize that communism must win out over capitalism through peaceful competition, by providing its people with a higher standard of living. To them this means that they are to enjoy *both* a rapidly rising standard of living at home and the peaceful spread of the Communist system abroad.

It is tempting to go beyond these undoubted changes in the atmosphere of Soviet society and to picture an unchanging and unending line of progression: "A better and better life at home, more indifference to the outside world and to what may happen in it; more and more freedoms at home, and less risk-taking abroad." It is one thing, however, to hope for or wish for a continuous lightening of the burdens that are borne by the Soviet people. It is quite another for a great power to base its policy on the assumption of an "inevitable" greater liberalization at home and more and more cooperation in world affairs. A great power cannot afford to base its own planning on any single set of assumptions except at the risk of foreclosing its freedom of future decision.

If or as the Brezhnev-Kosygin policies bring about improvements in Soviet society, they may conceivably strengthen the Soviet capacity to take vigorous action abroad. Nor is "a fat Communist" necessarily "a peaceful Communist." A "fat Communist," or a fat anyone else, is not inevitably a peaceful citizen of the world. Hitler's Germany was not driven to aggression by poverty, and India is hardly an example of aggressive ambition. A more flourishing and more powerful Soviet society may take up again the burden of spreading revolutionary faith. Whatever their discontents at home, Soviet people have a deep streak of pride, even arrogance, about Russia's role as a great power. On the whole, they agree with Khrushchev and his successors that no important question anywhere in the world can now be decided without the Soviet Union's having an important, and at times a decisive, voice. Most of the inside and informed criticism of Khrushchev's failures in foreign policy was directed, not at his attempts to use Soviet strategic and political power to make gains, but at his failure to bring them off, as in Berlin, the Congo, and Cuba. These blunders, and Peking's outspoken gloating over the Kremlin's discomfiture, raised the animosities between the two rivals to a shrieking pitch.

II

According to Marxist-Leninist theory, no such monstrosity as a rupture between two major centers of Communist power is conceivable. And yet it happened. The "inevitability" of the Sino-Soviet split seems easy enough to explain in retrospect. Yet apparently its inevitability was not clear at the time to either Nikita Khrushchev or Mao Tse-tung. Whatever its multiple origins, the fierce rivalry between Moscow and Peking has confronted Soviet policy makers with a great many unforeseen and presently insoluble problems.

One of these problems is directly related to the question of the role of infallible dogma in justifying Communist rule at home and in upholding Soviet prestige in world affairs. When each of two major and independent centers of Communist power insists that it alone possesses and propagates the sole correct version of Marxist-Leninist dogma, the way may be opened to perceiving dogma, not as an absolute and unchanging statement of goals, but rather as only one instrument of manipulation, a tool of some ulterior purpose. Thus the ideological confrontation between Peking and Moscow fosters indirectly that very spirit of skepticism, apathy, and relativism which is anathema to militant believers.

When Soviet policy makers think out loud to themselves, they must wonder why everything has gone awry in their China policy. None of the traditional explanations will do. Not even Agitprop has attempted to blame the U.S. Central Intelligence Agency for Peking's secession! If the Communist victory in China was such a great triumph for Marxism-Leninism and "proletarian internationalism," the Soviet leaders must also wonder sometimes how many similar "victories" they can afford. And the calm and unprovocative determination of non-Communist nations to shape their own futures must seem to the Kremlin both a reasonable and comfortably predictable factor in comparison with the hatred and vituperation that spew forth almost daily from Peking.

The Sino-Soviet split has greatly changed the position and role of Moscow within the Communist-ruled part of the world. Both in theory and in practice the Kremlin has conceded to the former satellites a degree of autonomy which they could hardly have dreamed of ten years ago. The quarrel has opened the way for even relatively small and weak parties to assert a substantial measure of independence, provided they acknowledge some degree of political and strategic reliance on the Soviet Union. No longer bound to the Soviet pattern in every detail, the former satellites in East Central Europe again take pride in their national glories of the past and their innovations of today. Indeed, one sure source of popularity at home is to demonstrate their attachment to the national culture through a variety of anti-Russian gestures. Communists in Warsaw and Budapest, and now also in Bucharest, disparage some of the

Soviet features of communism as evidence of "Russian backwardness" which could never happen "here."

Indeed, the new situation within the formerly "monolithic bloc" has resulted in a reverse flow of experimentation and cultural values into the Soviet Union. Even Western, nonruling Communist parties are contributing to the fresh flow of ideas. A large part of Moscow knows, for example, that the harsh sentences imposed on Andrei Siniavskii and Iulii Daniel in February 1966 evoked outspoken protests by prominent Communists in the West. Well-informed Soviet citizens are aware that the Communist Party of Great Britain has protested against the oppressive treatment of Jewish life and culture within the Soviet Union. A few of them may even know that Fidel Castro has openly poked fun at the Kremlin's obsessive fear of nonrepresentational painting and sculpture and modern music.

In their efforts to restore a façade of unity to as much as possible of the Communist-ruled part of the world, Brezhnev and Kosygin have faced the same problems as did their predecessor. After Khrushchev's dismissal the new leaders first sought in vain to build new bridges to Peking; they then sought and failed to secure a resounding condemnation of Communist China's disruptive strategy by a substantial number of strong parties. Their continuing lack of success in this elusive quest has been less obvious than Khrushchev's, chiefly because of the moderate and low-key manner in which they have pursued it.

The prestige of the new leadership has benefited, on the other hand, from the serious setbacks that have befallen Peking's ambitions, for example, in the Indonesia fiasco of late September 1965. Nevertheless, the Soviet leaders have failed to re-establish genuine and assured unity of action among Communist parties and regimes. They have had to reaffirm, perhaps with more conviction, Khrushchev's yielding of extensive autonomy to any party or regime that feels strong enough to assert the right to make its own decisions. Thus a ten-year struggle to retain a decisive influence over Communist

China has, by a curious twist of the dialectic, brought an unprecedented degree of autonomy to most Communist parties. At the same time it has largely dissipated the aura of monolithic unity and ideological infallibility which emanated from communism in Stalin's time. The effects on Communist prestige have been especially marked in the "third world," perhaps just because of the ten-year campaign by Moscow to exploit the hopes and resentments of former colonial peoples.

III

In contrast to Stalin, who, in his post-1945 quest for expansion, placed his main reliance on Soviet military strength, Khrushchev shifted the focus of his political strategy to the underdeveloped "third of mankind," in Asia, Africa, and Latin America. To back his policy, he developed a versatile arsenal of political weapons to be used in winning over the newly independent and economically less developed nations. As he saw it, the retreat of colonialism, first from Asia, then from Africa, presented a decisive opportunity to weaken Western capitalism and "imperialism." Under Khrushchev's leadership the Soviet Union rapidly expanded its efforts to encircle the "last stronghold" of capitalism in Western Europe and North America. The victory of Fidel Castro, and his decision to opt for "socialism" and Soviet protection, seemed for a time to spell the pattern of many other and even greater victories to come.

Yet nothing seemed to go right for Khrushchev or his successors. Except in Cuba, the "inevitable" progression of newly independent nations from colonial rule to political independence and then to the "higher stage" of socialist or pro-Communist regimes was not working out according to the Marxist-Leninist book. Even in the Cuban case, the economic and political costs of maintaining the Castro regime have run high, with no visible relief in sight. Since 1962 it has not been clear that Soviet policy would welcome any more "Cubas" at this time.

From the launching of Khrushchev's active policy in the "third world," the Kremlin has faced a basic dilemma, one which it has not yet resolved. What guarantees does Moscow have, apart from the somewhat tortuous assumptions of Marxism-Leninism, that its political and economic support will not strengthen and consolidate non-Communist regimes? Or that these regimes, once firmly in the saddle, will readily allow themselves to be dispossessed someday by definitely pro-Communist or even Communist forces?

This very real dilemma could be resolved, it was clear by 1960, in one of two ways. One was by thrusting aside the temporary nationalist and reformist allies as quickly as possible and as quickly improvising new Communist cadres to rule in their stead. Some of the heavy-handed Soviet efforts at remolding African and Asian students into bearers of Communist ideas — efforts that have frequently backfired in vehement protests — were launched with this in view. In much the same spirit of optimism the University of the East and the Lenin Schools had undertaken, in the 1920's, to prepare dedicated cadres to carry out future revolutions in Asia and elsewhere. The training of subversive cadres in Cuba, for use in Latin America, and in Ghana, for Africa, has been a grim sign of contemporary Communist preparations to "speed up the course of history."

Another, and quite different, way out of the dilemma was to accept non-Communist and anti-Western regimes as fully legitimate and to back them for an indefinite future. For this, too, there was strong precedent in Lenin's support for the Kemalist regime in Turkey. This course has meant accepting and backing "national democracies" as the most effective exponents of anticolonial nationalism and wooing them on their own terms through Soviet flattery and assistance. This new concept, which was promoted to a place of honor in Soviet policy by 1960, was first applied in Cuba and the former Belgian Congo. In neither situation did it work out as Moscow expected.

In the Congo (Léopoldville), Lumumba's hasty attempt to bring the country under Soviet protection led to widespread disorder, political and tribal conflicts, and United Nations intervention. In respect to Cuba, signals were badly crossed up in 1960 and 1961. Castro had proclaimed Cuba a "socialist state" in April 1961; presumably his regime was henceforth entitled, as a member in good standing of the socialist bloc, to demand full economic and strategic backing by Moscow. Soviet commentators, however, went on insisting that Cuba was still in the stage of "national democracy." In other words, Cuba was supposed to strengthen its defenses against "imperialism" and root out the domestic allies of the "imperialists," without being one hundred per cent committed to the Communist bloc or to Communist policies. Even in April 1962 Moscow's May Day slogans described Cuba as "building socialism," a stage antecedent to full "socialist" status. Thus in neither of its two major applications had the transitional concept of "national democracy" proved very useful to Soviet policy makers in defining either strategy or tactics toward the "third world."

Ever since 1960 Soviet policy in the developing countries had been greatly complicated by several other unforeseen problems, all of which have continued to plague Khrushchev's successors. One of the major questions has been what to do about "anti-imperialist" governments which receive large amounts of Soviet aid but which persecute their own Communists. The Egyptian case has been especially troublesome for Moscow ideologues. In this respect the visible results of the Khrushchev and Kosygin visits to President Nasser stand in sharp contrast. In May 1964 the then Soviet premier lectured his hosts in a most undiplomatic way on the fallacies of "Arab unity," the superiority of "scientific socialism" over "Arab socialism," and the need to undertake truly revolutionary changes within Egypt. On his return to Moscow, Khrushchev announced that the repression of Communists in Egypt had been ended. In May 1966, apparently, Premier Kosygin expressed no opinions, at least in public, on the domestic reforms or political goals of the Nasser regime. In the style of classical power politics he urged the formation of an alliance of "revolutionary" Arab states, to be led by the United Arab Republic and backed by the Soviet Union, and expressed cautious support for Egyptian ambitions in Yemen and South Arabia (Aden). Incidentally, Kosygin, unlike Khrushchev, did not announce or promise any new programs of Soviet aid; it is probable that the existing programs have several years to run and that the problem of securing the repayment of present debts now bulks larger in Kremlin eyes than it did in 1955 or even in 1964.

The Kosygin visit of May 1966 followed a rather strained period in Soviet-Egyptian relations. In January 1966 the U.A.R. government had brought to trial a group of alleged Communists, perhaps to balance an almost simultaneous court case against a group of alleged "Western agents." The Soviet press hastened to disavow any Soviet responsibility for Nasser's Communist opponents. It insisted that the persons accused were really adventurers who no longer had any right to use the name of communism, and it implied that responsibility for their conspiratorial actions rested squarely with Peking. In several other countries where Communist parties or groups have been suppressed by Moscow-backed nationalists, as in Indonesia, Iraq, and Algeria, the chief outward sign of Moscow's discomfiture has been an insistence that "true democrats," meaning Communists, should not be persecuted because they are "the most consistent fighters for freedom" and against imperialism.

IV

The problem of reconciling Communist long-range goals with Soviet support for non-Communist nationalist regimes has been compounded by the constant sniping and intrigues conducted by Communist China. In a variety of Afro-Asian organizations and meetings, beginning in 1960, Peking has attacked Moscow's support of non-Communist regimes as "opportunism" and "toadying to imperialism," indeed, as "entering into a conspiracy with the biggest imperialist of all," the

United States, to divide up the world. The shrill attacks by Peking on Moscow, and the more low-pitched denunciations of Chinese "adventurism" by Soviet spokesmen, have apparently provided a valuable educational experience for many nationalist leaders in the developing countries. President Nyerere of Tanzania has declared that his country is "not for sale," and has expelled a number of pro-Communist politicians from his administration. In Kenya, President Jomo Kenyatta rejected a large delivery of Soviet military equipment on the grounds that acceptance was conditional on the installing of a large Soviet military mission. In defense against Chinese Communist penetration of his ruling party, Kenyatta has accused several of his left-wing followers, especially Oginga Odinga, of using Peking subsidies to organize a coup against him and has expelled them from his party and from parliament. Elsewhere in Africa, in Dahomey, Upper Volta, the Central African Republic, and Ghana, military coups were followed, in late 1965 and early 1966, by the expulsion of all Chinese Communist personnel and by reducing the size of Soviet aid, information and other staffs. In 1966 two major institutes for Communist-style training of political cadres were disbanded by the governments of Kenya and Ghana. Thus both the militant Peking approach and Moscow's more gradualist policy have recently suffered important setbacks in several key countries of Africa.

Nevertheless, Soviet ideologists have continued their diligent efforts to reconcile Moscow's policy of "revolutionary internationalism" with the requirements of practical power politics. This has been done by reducing Soviet emphasis on the not very useful slogan of "national democracy" and placing greater stress on the promotion of "revolutionary democracy." This concept, introduced in Khrushchev's last months, was first applied to Guinea, Ghana (until Nkrumah's overthrow in February 1966), and Mali. Later, this accolade was applied for some time to Algeria, only to be withdrawn after the overthrow of Ben Bella in June 1965. It was bestowed in 1965 upon Burma and the Congo (Brazzaville).

"Revolutionary democracy" is the label that Moscow applies

to those countries which, in its estimate, are moving beyond the stage of "national democracy" and drawing steadily closer to Soviet policy. A regime thus praised is step by step achieving complete state control over its economy, thus eliminating gradually the last traces of "neocolonialism." Parallel with this evolution, the local one-party regime is expected to model its system of rule and propaganda more and more closely on the Soviet pattern and to enter into party-to-party intimacy, rather than merely government-to-government relations, with the Soviet Union. In accordance with this concept of ever-growing intimacy, groups of leading officials from several countries, including Mali and Congo (Brazzaville), have attended year-long courses of study at the Higher Party School of the Central Committee of the CPSU.

The Soviet expectation is that this penetration of several ruling parties, through molding the thinking of "leading cadres," will lead to a gradual, almost imperceptible, "growing over" of national liberation parties into the stage of "building the foundations of socialism," and eventually into the "building of socialism." Soviet theorists predict that, as nationalist leaders come to see the "superiority" of communism as a means of solving their problems of national development, they will spontaneously adopt more and more of the program and methods of "scientific socialism" and will lead their countries in the "socialist camp" without having to be displaced and destroyed by a new Communist-trained leadership emerging from below.

"Revolutionary democracy" is Moscow's retort to the Chinese Communist accusation that all its aid to non-Communist regimes is both politically wasteful and ideologically sinful. Instead of calling for the destruction of the nationalist regimes, in the Peking style of "continuous revolution," Moscow's slogan of "revolutionary democracy" is designed to remold nationalists into convinced supporters of "scientific socialism" and through them to carry out a peaceful transition to Communist rule. So far, it is true, this policy has not brought any concrete political gains. Yet the political concept is so flexible that it can, in theory, survive many setbacks and contradictions. For example, Mali, which has regularly received high marks in Soviet propaganda, is still heavily dependent on French subsidies, French officials, French trading companies, and French educators. And even Guinea, which has long headed the list of deserving "revolutionary democracies," receives 70 per cent of its foreign exchange earnings from FRIA, a Western bauxite consortium. Guinea has also taken steps which seem designed to regain the economic support of France and to seek the advantages of association with the European Economic Community. The gradualist approach has not brought Moscow any decisive gains, but it has enabled it to escape being implicated in Peking's fiascoes. The issue of force versus caution has been especially difficult for Moscow in the complex problem of Vietnam.

V

Since Khrushchev's dismissal, the expanding war in Vietnam has burdened Soviet policy with new problems. The Soviet leadership cannot lend its support to American proposals for a compromise settlement, for it must hope for and contribute to a victory by the Communists of North and South Vietnam. It cannot afford to leave a clear field to Peking's influence in Southeast Asia. On the other hand, a clear-cut Communist victory, if gained primarily by military means, would add great prestige to the Chinese Communist dictum that "political power grows out of the barrel of a gun."* It would stand out in stark contrast to the absence of new Soviet-sponsored victories elsewhere, despite Moscow's vastly greater economic and military power.

While much is said and written in the West about the prospective "Titoism" of Vietnamese communism, and of Hanoi's

*"Problems of War and Strategy, November 1938," in Mao Tse-tung, *Selected Military Writings* (Peking: Foreign Language Press, 1963), p. 272.

resistance to and fear of Peking's influence, it is speculative to assume that Ho Chi-minh or his successors would desire or be able, even with Soviet backing, to avoid acknowledging the preponderant role of its massive neighbor to the north. Whether Moscow is counting on the eventual withdrawal of U.S. forces from South Vietnam, or whether it would at some stage use what leverage it has to promote some sort of compromise or stalemate settlement between North Vietnam and a non-Communist regime in the south, is probably not known today even in the highest Soviet circles of policy making. What is certain is that any conceivable outcome is likely to cause serious damage to Kremlin interests and hopes. It is perhaps for this reason that the Soviet regime, while increasing its military and economic aid ever since Brezhnev's visit to Hanoi in January 1965, has, as under Khrushchev, avoided committing its strategic power or its political prestige to any clearly defined "solution." In response to both Western and neutralist soundings, the Kremlin has repeatedly indicated that only Hanoi can decide whether to soften its demand for the withdrawal of American power and the recognition of a Viet Cong regime. In the meantime the Soviet Union, which is not directly engaged in military combat anywhere, draws maximum psychological advantage from the predicament of the United States, which is fighting an undeclared war of great magnitude, at substantial cost, and for goals which, when defined, arouse little fervor at home and even less enthusiasm among its allies and friends.

The events in Indonesia since the abortive Communist coup of September 30, 1965, have been equally baffling to Soviet policy makers. The resort by Aidit and his party to violence and wholesale assassination offered circumstantial evidence of Chinese Communist inspiration and perhaps planning. The extremist coup must have been especially infuriating to Moscow because it cut short and reversed what had promised to be a major success story for Moscow's strategy of "revolutionary democracy." The Indonesian Communist Party, the largest in the world next to the Chinese and Soviet ruling parties, had seemed after 1963 to be on its way toward embracing and engulfing the governing regime, all with the blessing of Sukarno. The unexpected shift to violent revolution, Peking style, was not provoked by any hint that Sukarno might be preparing to abandon his increasing reliance on Communist support, and after the coup Bung Karno twisted and writhed in his efforts to preserve an organized Communist Party as an offset to the power achieved since October 1965 by the military leaders and their civilian allies. And it is far from clear that the military leadership in Indonesia, despite massive deliveries of Soviet military equipment, is inclined to listen to Soviet political advice.

The Kremlin has certainly welcomed the discredit that the abortive coup brought on Peking's "adventurist" policy. Yet, when anti-Communist forces gain the upper hand, as in the Indonesian case, they seem relatively indifferent to subtle distinctions among various brands of Communist doctrine. And the Indonesian adventure raised old ghosts elsewhere. Nasser's renewed persecution of Communists in 1966 was apparently stimulated by the shock which he felt at the bloody events in Djakarta. Several of the anti-Communist moves in Africa similarly reflect a high degree of alarm and revulsion at Chinese influence and purposes, and, to a lesser extent, at Communist goals and strategy generally.

Some of the same reaction may have influenced General Ne Win's decision to bring Burma back into contact with the West after several years of self-isolation. Only recently classified with Guinea and Mali as a "revolutionary democracy," Burma now appears determined to renew its economic and cultural ties with India, Japan, and the Western powers. It is too early, however, to judge whether this shift will be a lasting one, and whether it is due more to fear of what almost happened in Indonesia, or more to the belief that the United States is strongly and permanently committed to the containment of Communist expansionism in Southeast Asia. In any case even Burma now seems reluctant to act out the role that has been assigned to it by Soviet policy as a country "moving toward socialism."

VI

The complex and contradictory motives that shape Soviet policies in the "third world" were dramatically focused in the Tricontinental Congress, held at Havana in January 1966. Under the combined pressure of Chinese Communist and Castroite forces, the Congress took its stand in support of a militant policy of forceful subversion. With Soviet affirmative votes it set up a "liberation" committee which is to work out of Havana, to support and promote armed struggles for power beginning with Guatemala and Venezuela. Yet for several years Moscow has given strong support to moderate and gradualist Communist parties or factions, as in Chile, Brazil, and Mexico. In these and several other countries it has stressed the importance of the peaceful and parliamentary path to power, even through electoral and governmental alliances with socialist and other reformist parties.

The Havana Declaration of January 1966 placed the Kremlin in a very awkward position. Its promised support for subversion by armed minorities was sharply denounced in the Organization of American States and in the United Nations, and the spluttering disclaimers issued by the Soviet Ministry of Foreign Affairs could hardly plaster over the clear contradiction. The Brezhnev-Kosygin leadership has not resolved the inner contradiction of Soviet policy any better than Khrushchev, even though it has done a great deal to establish the image of a "responsible" Soviet government.

This reputation for political sobriety has been strengthened by the more cautious tone which has been continued by Khrushchev's successors and also by substantive shifts in the Soviet posture, as illustrated in the recent handling of the Kashmir, Cyprus, and Palestine problems. For more than a decade the Soviet government had given all-out support to the Indian claims in the Kashmir-Jammu quarrel, in contrast to the British, American, and United Nations efforts to promote a compromise settlement or at least a toning down of the conflict. This one-sided attitude, combined with Soviet backing for Afghanistan's claims to "Pushtoonistan," seemed designed to promote the destruction of Pakistan and to make India and Afghanistan dependent on Soviet support. Perhaps Peking's eager courting of Pakistan since 1962, together with its all too obvious desire to egg Pakistan on against India, was mainly responsible for Moscow's newly responsible and impartial attitude, culminating in January 1966 in Kosygin's active and useful mediation and the negotiation of the Tashkent Agreement. Certainly the Soviet interest in promoting a more stable balance in Asia and containing Peking's expansionism would hardly be served if India were to be weakened by Communist China or Pakistan and, even less so, if China and Pakistan were to ally themselves against India and dismember it.

In the dispute over Cyprus, both between Greek and Turkish Cypriots and between Greece and Turkey, Khrushchev almost instinctively chose a posture that would inflame and prolong the quarrel. His strong support for the Greek claims seemed designed to forestall what prospects there were for an early settlement. At the least his policy of exacerbating the conflict was certain to weaken the eastern flank of NATO, to eliminate the British bases on Cyprus, and possibly to promote neutralism in Greece and Turkey. Soviet threats against Turkey, in case the latter actually sent substantial forces to Cyprus, led to a U.S. warning to Turkey that NATO would not automatically come to its defense. This U.S. "underwriting" of the Soviet threat in turn set in train a substantial erosion of Turkish confidence in NATO and U.S. policy and led, for the first time since 1945, to a vigorous domestic discussion of the advantages of nonalignment.

As a result of the Turkish reaction to this disillusioning experience, and also as a consequence of intensive Soviet wooing of Ankara by the Brezhnev-Kosygin leadership, Soviet-Turkish relations are now on a friendlier footing than at any time since 1939. In the meantime, as many months pass, the possibility of the absorption of Cyprus by Greece or partition between Greece and Turkey steadily recedes. The consolidation of a weak but independent Cyprus, equipped with Soviet-bloc arms (in large part supplied through the United Arab Republic), and strongly influenced by a pro-Communist workers' party, represents a substantial plus to be chalked up to the credit of the cautious phase of Soviet foreign policy.

In the Palestine conflict Soviet policy has similarly moved a substantial distance, under Brezhnev and Kosygin, away from Khrushchev's ebullient fanning of extreme Arab hostility for Israel and toward a more impartial and responsible position. In his visit to Nasser in May 1966 Kosygin was careful not to lend Soviet public support to Arab demands for the destruction of Israel or for the creation of the Palestine Liberation Army. Soviet statements on other occasions have emphasized that the question of the "just claims" of the Arabs is not one that can safely be adjudicated by war.

Kosygin's speeches in Egypt did give strong support to President Nasser's proposals for an alliance of "revolutionary Arab states" — to include the United Arab Republic, Syria, Iraq, and the Republican regime in Yemen. Naturally Moscow would like to weaken British and American influence in Jordan, Saudi Arabia, and Kuwait, and would welcome the absorption of South Arabia and Aden into the Nasserite orbit after the forthcoming withdrawal of Britain from Aden, as announced by London in February 1966. Here, however, Soviet policy seems to be influenced more by considerations of power politics than of ideology. In the meantime its stance is calculated to strengthen nationalist allies and to assure them of Moscow's useful but unprovocative support against the West, rather than displaying an ambition to strive for direct ideological and political gains of its own.

This growing reluctance to choose sides hastily in the potentially countless conflicts of the "third world" is only one facet of a more complex process of scaling down the earlier expectations of easy and cheap political gains. As Khrushchev and Bulganin, in 1955, opened the first round of Soviet visits to the "third world" everything looked rosy. Now, almost twelve years later and many billions of rubles poorer, his successors are hard put to point to any concrete and acclaimable victories.

True, through providing large-scale credits to some nineteen countries and token credits to some twenty-five additional recipients, Khrushchev and his successors have won recognition everywhere that the Soviet Union is a strong industrial power and that its loans and its technology provide an alternative source, in addition to those of Western Europe, Japan, and the United States, for procuring manufacturing equipment of many kinds on a substantial scale. Through furnishing an alternative source of armaments the Kremlin has also competed with the West in strengthening a variety of military establishments, which may or may not contribute someday to promoting Soviet interests. No doubt this enhanced prestige, in areas of the world where little had previously been known about the Soviet Union or communism, has some potential value for Soviet policy.

Yet the gains have in part been offset by losses. Some of the Soviet-supported industrial projects have been carried out very efficiently and have won prestige and good will, as in India. Other projects have been poorly conceived. Some have had to be scrapped altogether because either power or raw materials or markets were not available. The high level of Soviet assistance to Cuba, the United Arab Republic, India, and Indonesia has led to widespread word-of-mouth grumbling at home, among the less and less patient Soviet public, and Khrushchev's successors have taken pains to emphasize to their people that the loans will be repaid in deliveries of consumer goods. Moscow has also become the target of numerous complaints by the less-favored applicants, who feel that their just claims to Soviet largesse have been slighted. At the United Nations Conference on Trade and Development, the Soviet Union barely escaped being pilloried as a selfish "have" nation along with the United States. The Soviet Union, like the United States, is discovering that in a world of needy and ambitious new states it may be less blessed to give than it had thought. And perhaps the Kremlin, too, has been surprised to discover that many of the leaders of newly independent countries have strong minds and strong wills of their own and intend to pursue their own aims as they see them, with or without development aid from the industrially advanced nations.

Soviet discussions of policy toward the "third world" have taken a more moderate turn since the Cuban missile crisis, and this trend has been emphasized more explicitly under the Brezhnev-Kosygin regime. Some Soviet commentators have pointed to the great mistake that some newly independent nations have made by hastily confiscating or nationalizing Western-owned industries, mines, and plantations, thereby depriving their countries of their main sources of foreign exchange earnings and of future development capital. Some Soviet publicists have stated plainly that the newly independent countries cannot possibly expect the Soviet Union to make good the great losses they would suffer through driving away Western investors. Sometimes they even advise the new governments to court Western private investment more actively and not to assume that the Soviet Union can afford to pay for their development programs. A few commentators have pointed out that premature or adventurous attempts to plunge into "socialist" experiments are likely to fail and thus discredit the whole idea of socialism and that the transition to "socialism" must, in any case, come at a relatively mature stage of development.

The wholesale deliveries of Soviet military equipment, like American and other arms deliveries, have raised the level of risks of war in many parts of the world. True, they have sometimes promoted Soviet purposes, for example, by buttressing India against Communist Chinese pressure and by helping Nasser weaken Western influences in the Arab world. On the other hand, Soviet arms deliveries to Somalia, with its irredentist claims to territories of neighboring states, has greatly alarmed Ethiopia and Kenya, each of which is more powerful and more influential than Somalia in African politics. The large deliveries to Indonesia, including jet planes and a battle cruiser, have so far brought no lasting political gains to Soviet policy.

More than ten years ago Khrushchev embarked on a risky and expensive policy of seeking to march the countries of the "third world" at double-quick time down the path to socialism, Soviet-style. Now his successors must wonder how they can find some way to limit these costly programs or make them provide some visible gains for Soviet policy. The mere promise that the Soviet consumer will someday receive export jams and canned fruit from Guinea is hardly an adequate return for the export of scarce resources. The Soviet honeymoon with the developing countries has been steadily subsiding from its peak of 1955–1962. What remains of it at present is a continuing and onerous obligation to support a variety of restless countries in the long and slow process of development, a process which may or may not follow political paths that will be congenial to Soviet ideology or Soviet interests.

VII

One source of Soviet moderation since late 1962 has been a realization, which was long resisted in the Kremlin, that the balance of power at present does not favor a policy of throwing its weight around. Another has been the realization that many things have happened, and many others may happen, which have not been predicted by the Marxist-Leninist book. A third has been a gradual decline in the confidence felt by the Soviet leadership in its ability to foretell and shape the future infallibly, in accordance with either its own ideology or its own wishful thinking. Increasingly, though reluctantly, the men in command of the Soviet regime seem less certain of their ability to drive that stubborn nag, History, down the road that their ideology and their messianic mission have supposedly marked out for her to follow.

Gradually but reluctantly, the Soviet leadership, both under Khrushchev and since, has accepted certain major facts as beyond its immediate or direct control. Among these facts is the great economic and strategic power of the United States, which is far greater than it was at the end of World War II. Another important fact is the striking economic revival and growth of Western Europe which is now far more productive and affluent than at any time in its history. Despite some contrary phenomena, Western Europe is also further advanced toward economic integration and political cooperation than at any time in the past. Another "fact" resides in the great complexities and uncertainties of the "third world," in contrast to the simplified and wishful picture that Soviet leaders, in their previous isolation, had painted of it. Recognition of these facts has been making the Soviet leadership less cocksure in its judgments and, it is hoped, will encourage it to be cautious in its actions.

Yet the moderate course of Soviet policy could be changed quite rapidly if either external conditions or the Kremlin's evaluation of those conditions should undergo a sharp alteration. For example, possible or conceivable changes in the strategic balance of terror might raise Moscow's currently modest expectations of what it could achieve by resuming the Khrushchev policy of bluster and nuclear threats. The Soviet Union is devoting great efforts to tipping the balance of nuclear-missile power in its favor. After it has completed the hardening of its missile sites and the strengthening of its command-and-control systems, the Soviet leadership may decide that it can risk bringing on a new confrontation, for instance, over Berlin or Cyprus. The improvement of Soviet multiple-warhead systems may lead it to the belief that it has offset the numerical superiority of the American Minuteman deterrent.

Another field of intense competition is that of antimissile systems. Since 1963 the Soviet government has repeatedly claimed — and similar claims have regularly been proved correct in the past — that it has solved the problem of the antimissile missile. Around several of its major cities it has been setting up systems that apparently belong in the antimissile category. The Soviet leadership has been actively developing both detection systems and killer submarines designed to counterattack the U.S. Polaris-missile submarines or at least compel them to operate at greater, and therefore less effective, distances from potential Soviet targets. Since early 1966 there has been a reinforced campaign to organize the cities for passive defense against missile attack; this is the priority mission of DOSAF, the very large civilian defense organization. All this suggests that the Kremlin does not regard the so-called nuclear stalemate of today as a desirable or permanent factor.

It is probable that there will be no single innovation as startling as the atomic or hydrogen bomb or the intercontinental missile. Yet it is conceivable that a whole series of relatively small changes in strategic technology may add up to give one side or the other of the balance a politically significant, perhaps a decisive, margin of power.

To a great extent the currently popular and complacent projections of Soviet policy into a more and more passive and even benevolent and cooperative future rest on the assumption that a plateau of bipolar stalemate has now been reached and that this relatively stable state will never again be upset. The history of military technology in recent decades and the extremely tense race for superiority in military technology make this assumption, at best, a fragile one. If Soviet policy was so demanding and threatening at a time of clear strategic inferiority, it is not reassuring to contemplate what its new posture may be, should it achieve a clear-cut and recognized position of superiority, or even of equality. A favorable turn in the strategic competition — that is, favorable to Soviet strength — could conceivably lead to a revived assertion of Soviet claims to new political gains.

A second potential stimulus to a more aggressive posture on the part of the Kremlin might come from the dissolution of NATO and the withdrawal of U.S. strategic protection from Western Europe. Despite its repeated disappointments the Soviet leadership has never deviated one iota from the view that Western Europe is crucial to its hopes for a decisive victory. After World War II Stalin assumed, mistakenly, that the United States would shortly withdraw from the affairs of Europe, leaving it to flounder in economic misery, social despair, and political impotence. From this basic mistake flowed many of the blunders, rages, and defeats of Soviet postwar policy. While the Kremlin now takes a more sophisticated view of American policy toward Western Europe, it also looks impatiently for the weakening of American influence in Europe. When President de Gaulle implies, in Paris or Moscow, that Europe's problems must be settled by "Europeans," Moscow applauds with enthusiasm the implication that the Soviet Union is a "European" power and that the United States is not.

Moscow would, of course, like to be rid of both European integration and NATO, so that it would then be free to make individual and one-sided arrangements with each of a congeries of small or medium European states, each jealous and suspicious of its neighbors. Somehow, Moscow does not really believe in the early advent of this best (for it) of all possible Europes. But naturally it will do what it can to enlarge and exploit any fissures that may appear within Western Europe or between Western Europe and America. And it will have the means at hand to resume its former pressures against Western Europe if it decides someday that the fissiparous trends in the Atlantic world have reached a point of no return. Prolonged weakness and division of purposes in the West would lead, eventually if not immediately, to a revival of Soviet ambitions and enticements.

Still another source of a more aggressive Soviet posture might be a reconciliation between Moscow and Peking. Clearly Moscow hopes against hope that sooner or later, perhaps after the demise of Mao Tse-tung, Communist China will recognize that its long-range hopes for economic, military, and political strength require that it cooperate with Russia for a long time to come, perhaps for several decades. Moscow still hopes that a younger, postrevolutionary leadership in Peking will make what would be, in practice, relatively small ideological concessions in order to restore the Sino-Soviet alliance to full vigor. Perhaps the purges of mid-1966 reflect Mao's fears that more moderate successors may be tempted to abandon his quixotic attempt to challenge both the United States and the Soviet Union at one time.

In any case, a reconciliation between Moscow and Peking, should it occur, would mean that the Kremlin would be obliged to commit Soviet power — economic and strategic — to the pursuit of agreed joint aims. And those purposes could only be advanced at the expense of the West, for example in Asia and Africa. Thus the requirements of a Sino-Soviet reconciliation — which Moscow must continue to seek in order to recover its lost aura of infallible leadership — might lead the Soviet leadership to adopt a more militant stance in Asia and perhaps more generally in the "third world." This turn of events could lead to new alarums and excursions, and to a variety of wars by proxy in the turbulent areas that lie between the South Atlantic and the Sea of Japan.

The foregoing reflections do not constitute a prediction, even less a timetable. But they should remind us both that the means available to give effect to Soviet ambitions will surely not remain static over the next two or three decades and that the opportunities offered to those ambitions by future events, whether or not they unfold under Soviet control, may be both varied and tempting.

The Soviet Union is a powerful state of a new type. Its very existence at home and its influence abroad are based upon a deepset stratum of revolutionary ambition and messianic romanticism. Its leaders and its influential people believe that Russia must have a very strong voice, at times a decisive voice, in whatever happens anywhere on the globe. Its leaders believe that the Western system of power, maintained increasingly by the almost unaided efforts of the United States, cannot resolve the multiple and intractable problems of world politics and that opportunities to apply the Communist formula in new areas will arise sooner rather than later.

Under Khrushchev's successors the Soviet government has shown greater realism in appraising the complex problems it sees everywhere. It seems somewhat more objective in analyzing the balance of political influence. It has been more cautious in injecting its power into complex and unfamiliar situations. Possibly, Brezhnev and Kosygin and their successors may find the line of moderation so fruitful abroad and so comfortable at home that they will pursue it for some years or even several decades, until it becomes a matter of enduring habit. Or, on the other hand, after making a fresh appraisal of the power balance and available opportunities, they may set about refurbishing Russia's role as a revolutionary great power. Since Khrushchev's dismissal the new leadership has moved steadily to reap the political benefits of a policy that had become, in practice, a cautious and moderate one. At the same time it has been careful not to foreclose any of the expansionist options of Soviet policy, against the time when it may succeed in tipping the strategic and political balance in favor of a renewed messianic urge.

THE FOREIGN POLICY OF COMMUNIST CHINA

GEORGE E. TAYLOR

An examination of the nature of Communist society in China as well as of the record since 1949 suggests that Peking pursues three main foreign-policy objectives. The first is to strengthen and extend the political power and authority of the Communist state. Because Peking has absorbed the Tibetans and Mongols and re-established spheres of influence in Korea and Southeast Asia, this objective appears on the surface to be nothing more than the foreign policy of any great power — in this case an effort to restore the ancient glories of China. There are clearly many aspects of Peking's policy that parallel those of a conventional great power, but the comparison is superficial. The dynamics of the power structure of a Communist regime demand territorial and political expansion but in a very special context. Like the Russian Communists, the Chinese Communists have an attitude toward the state, nationalism, power, and "national interest" which stems from a specific ideological base. Chinese Communist imperialism is essentially the same as that of the Soviets.

The second objective of Communist China is to seek to influence, possibly eventually to dominate, the policies of the Communist world. In its present phase this involves a struggle with the Communist Party of the Soviet Union and a campaign for organizational support in Communist parties in every part of the world. The noisy and dramatic aspects of the Peking-Moscow split conceal the fact that the struggle for power is built into the Communist system. The personal struggles that began with the birth of the Chinese Communist Party took second place to party-versus-party and state-versus-state conflicts after 1949, when China began to build "socialism in one country" in Asia after the attempted general revolution in colonial Asia initiated in 1948 had failed to materialize.

The third objective is to shift the world balance of forces in favor of the Communist bloc of states, an objective shared with the Soviet Union but one which Peking would prefer to guide according to its own ideas. Peking, in fact, appears to be trying to use the Soviet Union in its effort to promote the revolution in Asia, just as Moscow attempted, after 1923, to use China to conquer Europe. All three objectives are closely connected, and although they are stated in sequence for purposes of analysis, no order of priority is implied.

The three objectives sometimes conflict. There are times when Peking has seemed to put the struggle with Moscow ahead of other considerations and has been forced to pay for this choice with considerable strain on the economy and the risks attendant on disunity within the bloc. Actually, Peking, in its own view, is still pursuing all three objectives at the same time. Short-term losses are sacrificed to long-term gains. It is the dynamics of Chinese Communist Party politics that determine strategy and tactics and provide the key to the relative emphasis which is put on the pursuit of each objective.

The present balance of military force in the world, especially the nuclear stalemate, may not be permanent, but it has for the time being practically ruled out unlimited wars between great powers. It is not surprising therefore that limited wars in which conventional weapons are used have assumed greater importance. The most significant type of limited war, however, is an old Communist-style type of war, now called the war of national liberation, which has been adapted to contemporary conditions and brought to a high level of sophistication, especially in Vietnam. This type of war is the main technique employed by both the Soviet Union and Communist China to take over control of the "third world" and thus shift the balance of world power against the West without involvement in nuclear destruction.

I

One of the first acts of the Communist rulers of China after acquiring control over the mainland was to commit the Party and the country to a radical departure in foreign policy. Mao Tse-tung announced that the foreign policy of China would be based upon the slogan "lean to one side," in other words, a complete commitment to the Communist world. In spite of the later friction with the Soviet Union, this policy still stands. Other Asian nations had taken other roads. India under Nehru followed a neutralist course which at times, at least from the Western point of view, appeared to be somewhat favorable to the Communist world but avoided entangling alliances of any sort. The same was true of Burma and Indonesia, countries which, unlike China, had long been under Western imperial rule. Why then did not the Chinese Communists retain their freedom of action? That they did not do so suggests that the decision to identify China with the fortunes of the Communist world was dictated by the character and needs of the new government.

The main factor was that a Communist party had come to

power, not a nationalist party as in India or Indonesia, and that this party was beginning the long process of establishing new forms of power and new ways of ruling China which were expected to arouse the hostility of the non-Communist powers. It is possible that the Party leaders thought of the early years of Bolshevik rule in Russia, when the new regime had to fend off the White armies which had the help of British, French, Japanese, and American intervention. The Chinese Communists apparently assumed that they would have to protect themselves from a similar fate and that the only possible ally would be the Soviet Union. This first decision to lean to one side would have been inconceivable without the unique factor of a Communist take-over of the mainland of China.

To analyze the foreign policy of a large country is no easy task. In the case of China it is complicated by the difficulties of obtaining certain kinds of information. Some observers seem to feel that the lack of information is so great that we should go to almost any length to secure for Americans, especially journalists, the privilege of traveling on the Chinese mainland. How serious, then, is this lack of information? I think we can justly claim that the United States is better informed about Communist China today than is any other country in the free world. If we judge by the numbers of well-trained scholars, the amount of instruction offered, the library resources, scholarly publications, and money invested in the study of China, then the total resources of the countries of Western Europe amount to a mere fraction of those of the United States. It is true that American scholars do not go to Communist China. Nor does it further this particular point to say that they are prevented only by the refusal of Peking to allow them in. The obstacles are not on this side. Although there is no substitute for being on the ground, most of the correspondents and scholars from other countries who have resided in Communist China are quite frank about their difficulties and frustrations. Diplomats tell us that Hong Kong is a far more valuable source of information about Communist China than is Peking. Nor is it essential to have diplomatic relations with a country in order to exchange visitors. Japan, which does not recognize Communist China, has permitted its citizens to go by the thousands to that country. Canada does not recognize Communist China, but some Canadians are permitted to go there. The main difficulty in obtaining information on mainland China stems not from the fact that Americans are not allowed to visit there but from the extraordinary efforts made by the Communist regime to prevent both its own and other peoples from knowing those things it wishes to conceal. Our experience with the Soviet Union shows that even when we have diplomatic relations and scholarly exchanges, the measures taken by a Communist regime to guard its decision-making processes are quite successful. We have to conclude therefore that unless there is a radical change in the attitude of the Chinese Communist regime, it is doubtful that access to the mainland would add a great deal to the information we have now.

The important thing is the kind of information we are looking for. Those who speak most about our ignorance of China are thinking perhaps of the sort of information that is readily available in an open, pluralistic society such as our own and is relevant to the discussion of foreign affairs because foreign policy is greatly influenced by public opinion and open discussion. The tendency is to look for this sort of information in other countries, whether Communist or not, and to feel frustrated if the information is not easily available. In Communist countries this sort of information is either nonexistent or for the most part irrelevant. There is no public discussion of the kind to which we are accustomed because there is no public responsibility for the making of foreign policy or even for the choice of those who make it.

There is a type of information that is sometimes underplayed by those who speak constantly about the need for further information. This is information about the nature and character of a Communist government and society. Although more research is needed, we have gained a good deal of insight into the character of Communist states — some of it from the record, some of it from those who have escaped from such states, and some from the public declarations and stated objectives of Communist governments. The question is the degree to which this knowledge is relevant to foreign policy. There are many who would argue that the internal political arrangements of a great state are not of decisive importance because the state has to behave pretty much like any other state when it comes to matters of territory, access to economic resources, military security, and prestige. The national interest, it is urged, is something that everyone understands because it is based on nationalism, which is assumed to be a constant. Those who urge this point of view would agree that when a revolutionary movement is at its height, actions are taken in the field of foreign affairs that do not fit in with the normal pattern. But revolutions, it is argued, tend to wear themselves out, and if they are successful the revolutionaries of yesterday become the conservatives of today. It is suggested that our present relations with the Soviet Union have a sort of stability that is due partly to the balance of terror but also to changes within Soviet society. As the Communists put on fat, according to this theory, they acquire a democratic dislike for muscle. They have achieved so much that they are unwilling to risk losing it by war. It is ironical that the argument comes back to the domestic situation, as well it might, for this is the heart of the matter.

The term "nationalism" is no key to domestic politics. The social and political content of nationalism is determined in the final analysis by the institutional power configuration of a country. That is why the foreign policy of imperial China was so different from that of George III, and even more from that of George Washington. There has always been nationalism in China, but not until modern times was it associated with changes in the social and political structure that under Chiang Kai-shek gave it some of the texture of Western nationalism or under Mao Tse-tung of Communist-style nationalism. The case of China permits us to compare two brands of nationalism in modern times — that of the present National Government of China and that of the People's Democratic Republic. The point is well worth examining because one of the arguments presented in the recent Fulbright hearings was that the behavior of the Chinese Communists today can be partly explained by the reaction of the Chinese to a century of humiliation at the hands of the imperialist powers.

What are the facts? The Kuomintang took over the government of China in 1928 and lost control of the mainland in 1949. During that period it can be properly suggested, I think, that the Kuomintang, certainly up to the middle of World War II, expressed a kind of Chinese nationalism which, but for the war, might well have been associated with a pluralistic, multi-centered society, with certain liberal democratic features. The hold of the Kuomintang on the Chinese people was strong enough to carry them through the war and enable them to resist all temptation to come to terms with the Japanese. Step by step the National Government had acquired full territorial and administrative integrity for China. On May 20, 1943, the "unequal treaties" came to an end. The United States was not only accepted but welcomed as an ally. The Kuomintang followed an independent nationalist policy in the war with Japan, accepting help at one time from the Soviet Union and later from the United States.

Compare this sort of nationalism with that of the Communists. If the National Government were now in control of the mainland, we might have difficulties with it, but it is very doubtful that it would be sponsoring the Viet Cong or fomenting trouble in Asia and Africa and Latin America, or making the United States the scapegoat for all its troubles. It is communism, not nationalism, that calls for the hate campaign against the United States, for the militarization of a quarter of the people of the earth, for the racial invective, and for the support of revolutionary movements in Southeast Asia, Africa, and Latin America. Without making any value judgment, we can clearly see that the two kinds of Chinese nationalism that are now in opposition to each other are very different.

Nothing stands out in such sharp contrast as the China of 1937 and the China of today. Under the National Government there was a constitution that promised an eventual fulfillment of democracy, a mixed economy, an educational system based on free and open access to the intellectual currents of the rest of the world, and diplomatic relations with all other states. Under the Communists we have the usual features of the Communist state, a nonhereditary, self-perpetuating party with no commitment to democracy in our sense, an educational system based on a single, dogmatic intellectual position and closed to all others, state control of all forms of intellectual expression as well as of economic activity, and a diplomacy based upon a division of the world along Communist and non-Communist lines. Such a state has to control the access of its population to information and foreign contacts; unless there are basic changes in its political structure, it must either isolate itself from the thought and institutions of the Free World or eventually reduce them to impotence. The Communist regime is willing to exploit the past for propaganda purposes, but its purposes and philosophy represent a complete break with Chinese tradition.

II

The important thing about international relations is what is related. In examining the three main objectives of Chinese Communist foreign policy it is essential to keep in mind that the integrating principle stems from the character of the Chinese Communist state. We know quite a lot about the main features of the Communist state in China, but we do not yet know enough about Communist states in general to be able to assess the significance of the changes that have already taken place or predict those that are yet to come. But decisions have to be made on the basis of present understanding, and premises must therefore be stated. In the 1930's Winston Churchill, on the basis of political instinct, insisted that there was no way of dealing with Hitler except by force. Douglas Miller, in his now forgotten book *You Can't Do Business with Hitler*, gave a sound and rational presentation of the same thesis. There is no intention to argue by analogy, because there are sharp differences between Hitler's Germany and Mao's China. But all the evidence goes to show that Communist states are also intent on shifting the world balance of forces in their favor.

The point becomes clear when we examine the first objective of Chinese Communist foreign policy, the extension of political power and authority. If this is a restoration of ancient glories, then the question that arises is, which period in imperial China do we take as the norm? Do we think of the frontiers of China under the conquest dynasties of the Mongols or the Manchus or under the Ming? Are we speaking of Chinese nationalism or Chinese imperialism — of the eighteen provinces or the Chinese empire? While the United States, historically, has shared in the privileges of the imperial powers in China, it has not sought Chinese territory and during World War II tried to build Nationalist China into a great power, making that objective an important part of its foreign policy. What is there, then, about Chinese Communist foreign policy that demands that all United States influence be rejected in the western Pacific? The record seems to suggest that the Chinese Communists are interested in much more than the restoration of even the farthest borders of the earlier Chinese state; their expansionism is of a specific order.

In the last letter he wrote, which was to Paul Goodman, Adlai E. Stevenson pointed out that the new Communist "dynasty" has been very aggressive. "Tibet was swallowed, India attacked, the Malays had to fight twelve years to resist a 'national liberation' they could receive from the British by a more peaceful route. Today, the apparatus of infiltration and aggression is already at work in North Thailand. Chinese maps show to the world's chagrin the furthest limits of the old empire marked as Chinese. I do not think the idea of Chinese expansionism is so fanciful that the effort to check it is irrational."

What type of aggression is this? Surely it combines all three characteristics of Chinese Communist foreign policy. Political support of a terrorist movement in Malaya, the intervention in Korea, the assistance given to the Vietminh immediately after the conquest of the mainland, the training and supply of cadres for the Free Thai movement, the pressures on Laos and Cambodia, serve to appeal to Chinese chauvinism (thus outbidding the National Government) as well as to shift the balance of world power in favor of Communist states and to improve the bargaining position of Communist China as against that of the Soviet Union. In 1948 it was the Cominform rather than China that played a decisive role in a general Communist effort to take over the new nations of South and Southeast Asia, by means of coordinated moves in India, Burma, Vietnam, Indonesia, and the Philippines. If it had succeeded, it would have brought Communist power to the Straits of Malacca and at one blow have seriously shifted the balance of forces in that part of the world. It was the Soviet Union that initiated the attack on South Korea, the climax of this offensive, but it was China that took advantage of Soviet miscalculation to make her first significant move by sending in "volunteers."

Communist China was in no danger of invasion from Tibet. The crime of the Tibetans was that they wished to be independent and non-Communist. The reason for demolishing Tibetan hopes for independence was to extend Communist political power, deny Tibet to other powers, and to acquire a strategic position from which to influence the affairs of South Asia.

What of the intervention in the Korean conflict? There are those who argue that the Chinese volunteers moved into North Korea because Peking was concerned about the safety of its own frontiers rather than the preservation of the North Korean regime. Both may be true. Peking may well have believed that United Nations forces would cross the Chinese frontier although they had no evidence to support their belief. Earlier in the war it had been given assurance by President Truman that the Seventh Fleet would prevent any invasion of the mainland from Taiwan or vice versa. It is more likely that the Chinese Communists intervened in the Korean conflict in order to preserve the North Korean Communist Party, an action fully in accord with the stated operational code of the Communists. There is no reason to suppose that Macao and Hong Kong are not on the list for annexation. Both could be taken almost overnight, and both were formerly parts of Chinese territory, but they apparently have a lower priority than did Malaya or Laos and Cambodia and Vietnam and presently are, no doubt, regarded as useful windows to the West. Considerations other than those of rounding out the territories of the old Chinese state obviously entered into the timetable.

The conquest of Taiwan is an overriding objective of the Chinese Communists, more because it is a rival center of power than for the territory. That is why the policies of the United States and Communist China come into the sharpest conflict in regard to the future of the National Government of China. The United States has been actively involved in the Chinese civil war, in the conflict between the Republic of China and the People's Democratic Republic, ever since the Korean War when President Truman interposed the Seventh Fleet between Taiwan and the mainland. Although President Eisenhower "unleashed" Chiang Kai-shek, the fact remains that United States policy does not include support of Chiang Kai-shek in recovering the mainland any more than it admits of the possibility of forceful conquest of Taiwan by Peking.

In the period between the conquest of the mainland and the opening of the Korean War, the United States was moving slowly toward the recognition of the new regime and had made it quite clear that it would not give any assistance to the National Government of China in the event of a Communist attack. Preparations for such an attack were actually in process but were canceled mainly because of the incidence of disease in the armies which were being trained on the mainland for invasion. There is some evidence also that the attack was postponed in order to back up, if necessary, the invasion of South Korea. Whatever the reason, the fact remains that the Korean War was the occasion, if not the cause, of the present United States policy with respect to the government of the Republic of China.

There are actually some advantages to Peking in keeping this issue alive but there is no doubt that from Peking's point of view the matter has to be settled sooner or later. As the United States has decided that it must be settled by peaceful means, the Communists are continuing the struggle on that basis both in the United Nations and in the forum of American public opinion. If the United Nations can be brought to accept the credentials of Peking as those of China, then the prestige of Nationalist China would be dealt a blow that would create serious demoralization in Taiwan and possibly prepare the ground for a take-over. If the Taiwan issue could be settled to the mutual satisfaction of Peking and the United States, a highly unlikely event, the question arises whether this would remove the main irritant and permit a normal relationship between the two countries. It is not very likely. It is well to remember that the cold war with the Soviet Union began after several years of ceaseless efforts on the part of the United States to cooperate in the prosecution of the war and the establishment of the peace. The Korean conflict finally ended in compromise and armistice but in no improvement of relations. The political appeal of Nationalist China to the overseas Chinese should not be underestimated, but it is certainly not strong enough now to be of decisive political concern to Peking. Unless and until it should become so, Peking may have more to gain than to lose by keeping the Taiwan issue alive until the time it can be settled under conditions of maximum humiliation to the United States.

One danger in the hypothesis that the foreign policy of China can be explained mainly in terms of old-fashioned nationalism and great-power politics is that it implies that there is always a possibility of compromise and mutual understanding between great powers. This hypothesis does not explain the Communist Chinese policy toward Japan and toward nuclear armament. If the hundred years of humiliation are to be accepted as the mainspring of Peking's nationalism, then surely the Japanese, to say nothing of the Russians, should come in for considerable attention. Japan clearly has all the characteristics of an imperialist power if Peking so wishes to paint her: the democratic institutions, the capitalist economy, and the imperialist past.

The contrast between the affluence of Japan and the poverty of China must be obvious to all. The two powers could get along on a great-power basis because Japan is almost disarmed, but the record shows that Peking's policy is to manipulate the internal politics of Japan in such a way as to separate Japan from the United States and consolidate a neutralist attitude.

Peking's interest in the development of nuclear power is usually explained as arising from the fear of a United States nuclear strike and invasion. If Peking had nuclear capacity it would leave Peking freer to establish its hegemony in Asia and give support to "people's wars." Those who argue this way also point out that the Chinese are well aware of the destructiveness of nuclear weapons and of what would happen to mainland China if the United States were to use them against it. The Communists realize that everything they have would be destroyed and that the Party would have to retreat into the hinterland and begin all over again. Hence they are determined not to take any action that would invite American nuclear attack.

Thus, the first objective of Peking's policy, to expand the political power and authority of the Communist state, is a complex phenomenon that is both Nationalist and Communist. The second main characteristic, the drive for a controlling position among the Communist powers, arises from the very nature of communism. There have been struggles for power within the Communist world from the very beginning, the most notorious of which was that between Stalin and Trotsky. As is customary in the Communist world, a struggle for personal power was expressed in ideological terms. On the face of it the quarrel was merely a difference of interpretation and of policy. Actually the winner would determine the current and correct definition of the truth.

III

The conflict between Peking and Moscow has many of the same features. After the death of Stalin, Mao Tse-tung apparently considered himself the senior Communist theoretician in the world and the natural heir to the throne. To the personal element, which was perhaps predominant in the Stalin-Trotsky issue, there is now added the conflict between the two great decision-making centers and state organizations. This is not an ordinary conflict between two allies, two nation-states that have fallen out over matters of rival claims to territory or broken promises; this is a very special kind of conflict which started within the family and continued within the family. Even if the family breaks up, the members still have much in common, more perhaps than either has with any other nation of the world.

There are several reasons for the split. One is that the Chinese came to realize that in spite of Russian assistance in building the means for creating nuclear power, Moscow intended to keep control over the use of nuclear weapons. It is also possible that Peking discovered that Moscow was not willing to assist in putting pressures on the United States to stay out of a battle of wills for the elimination of Nationalist forces on Quemoy and Matsu and for a possible invasion of Taiwan. Another factor of some importance seems to be the fear in Peking that Moscow, under pressure to come to arms-control agreements with the United States to regulate the use of nuclear weapons, might be tempted into further agreements with the United States that would blunt the edge of Soviet support in pressing for revolutionary changes in the world balance of forces. Peking also complained about the relative amount of economic assistance that the Soviet Union has given to India and other neutrals compared to that given to Communist China. Of even greater significance perhaps has been the tendency of the Soviets to make policy decisions affecting the whole Communist world without taking the Chinese Communists into full consultation. There were many examples of this — the most serious being the Khrushchev attack upon Stalin at the 20th Congress of the Soviet Party in 1956.

The attack on Stalin put Mao in a very difficult position, for while Khrushchev had someone to blame for past mistakes and terrorism, there was no one for Mao to blame except himself.

At first the Chinese Communist Party tried to adjust itself to the new anti-Stalin line by adopting a new constitution which emphasized Marxism-Leninism over the thought of Mao Tse-tung and by making a gesture toward the new collective leadership by enlarging the Central Committee of the Communist Party. Gestures were also made toward an emphasis on the rule of law, which would include the establishment of limits on the arbitrary actions of the Party, and toward the desirability of raising the living standards of the people.

Going along with the spirit of the changes in the Soviet Union, the Chinese Communist leaders said some brave words about improving the treatment of the intellectuals by giving them more respect and better conditions of work. The crude methods of the Thought Reform drive would give way to a more subtle approach. Out of this came the so-called Hundred Flowers Movement, spurred on perhaps by the Hungarian uprising in 1956, which had encouraged those in China who were not satisfied with the Communist Party. In a speech of February 1957 Mao Tse-tung himself admitted that mistakes had been made and that he would welcome criticism, within the framework of Marxism-Leninism. If there was anyone to blame for the mistakes which had been made in the ideological remolding of the Chinese people, they had been made not by Mao but by his subordinates.

It was the intention of Mao Tse-tung to control whatever criticism was to be permitted and guide it into constructive channels. The attempt failed. All over the country criticism of the Communist Party and attacks on its leaders spread rapidly. Students in particular played an important role in attacking Communist Party officials and Communist cadres. By June 1957 the counterattack began, and those who had criticized the Party were now condemned in mass meetings and forced to denounce themselves in humiliating confessions. Some were executed. It was clear that there was a tremendous amount of hostility to the Communist regime even among the students at the elite universities. Communist China was in no position to relax any controls. Revisionism became the chief enemy of the state. Discipline and control had to be re-established with ruthless and relentless purpose. Faced with political crisis and economic shortages, Mao Tse-tung quite typically tried to solve his problem with bold, politically inspired measures. While intensifying the drive to control the intellectuals, Mao instituted the commune system in agriculture in order to overcome the shortage of capital and to speed up agricultural production. There was to be a Great Leap Forward in industrialization. This movement began in 1958. By the end of 1959 it had resulted in economic disaster and a retreat from the extreme measures that had been taken.

The most important retreat was the ideological retreat. To understand this, we have to recall some other factors in Sino-Soviet relations. Now that there was more than one Communist state in the world, the problem had arisen of how doctrinal truth for the whole movement should be arrived at. The machinery for doing this within a single party was clear enough, but there was no machinery for the movement as a whole. The Comintern had gone in 1943, the Cominform in 1956. The Soviet Union had given up the claim to being the "center" of the world Communist movement in 1957 and promised to treat all Communist parties on the basis of equality. Soviet leadership now depended upon a claim to having advanced furthest on the way to world communism. The Soviet Union was the vanguard of the movement. When Mao Tse-tung claimed therefore that his communes and the Big Leap Forward put China ahead of the Soviet Union on the road to communism, he was attacking the legitimacy of Soviet leadership.

The Soviet reaction was vigorous, and the Chinese had to retreat from their ideological claims. At a famous meeting held at Lushan in July 1959, it appeared that there was a deep struggle within the Chinese Communist Party, and an effort was made to get rid of Chairman Mao, who had already resigned as Chairman of the Republic. Mao actually came out victorious, purged his competitors, and without resuming the chairmanship reasserted his undisputed leadership of the Party and the country. From that time on there seems to have been no possibility of reconciliation between Mao and Khrushchev or his successors. It is possible that an element of megalomania on the part of Mao Tse-tung now became a factor in the situation. The cult of personality came back again, and the thought of Mao Tse-tung became the dominant thought of the country — an answer to all problems and a cure apparently for all ills. One statement in January 1960 read: "Comrade Mao Tse-tung is the most outstanding representative of the proletariat in our country, and the greatest revolutionary leader, statesman, and theoretician of Marxism-Leninism in the present era." This is typical of many statements that can be found in the Peking *People's Daily*. The Soviet Union, presumably in answer to Chinese claims and attacks, withdrew its technical advisers from China and cut down on trade and aid.

The organizational struggle between Moscow and Peking now reached new heights of invective and maneuvering. The Soviets still clung to the position that they owed their leadership to the claim that the Soviet Union was farthest on the road to communism, while the Chinese tried to institutionalize Soviet leadership in such a way that the Soviets could be held responsible and therefore be attacked. The Chinese, far from wishing to destroy the unity of the Communist movement, wanted to strengthen it in the hope that eventually they could take it over. In the Aesopian dialogue that filled so many communications, each side accused the other of practically the same deviations. In fact there is little, as far as policy toward the rest of the world is concerned, on which there was any difference. Both are on the record as supporting the doctrine that war is "not fatally inevitable," that all Communist states must support national liberation revolutions both through armed struggle and nonmilitary efforts, and that there should be a double strategy of illegal and legal means of promoting communism in capitalist countries as well as in the rest of the world. Behind the scenes the Soviet Union sought to establish its control over China by withholding economic aid while promising to renew it if the Chinese were to give up their attacks and agree to a Soviet-dictated resolution of the organizational struggle. All this means that while a break in party or state relations is always possible, the opposite is also not unlikely.

In this struggle the Chinese acquisition of nuclear power has its place. Acquisition of a nuclear capability is designed to increase China's prestige not only with the West but also with the Soviet Union and the rest of the Communist world.

IV

The third objective of Chinese policy, to shift the balance of world forces in favor of the Communist states, is one to which any Communist state must of necessity subscribe. From the Communist point of view the erosion of the prestige and influence of the Free World is the only real guarantee for the security of the Communist system of domestic power. They must eliminate competition of every sort on the international as on the domestic front — for the same reasons. If the Communist parties do not succeed in this, they will have to face changes in political structure which they are not willing to accept. This view is challenged by those who advance the comforting thought that all revolutions burst out with exuberant energy and then quiet down into mellow and harmless phenomena. The French Revolution, which is usually given as an example, is not even a good example, for the French revolutionary imperialism was stopped only by defeat at the Battle of Waterloo, not by "mellowing." The dynamics of one-party dictatorship admit no modification of political structure or objective; they can be restrained only by superior political and military forces.

The Chinese Communists use the goal of the victory of communism throughout the world to their advantage in opposing the leadership of the Soviet Union. Mao Tse-tung, not being the leader of a great power, can call for measures far more aggressive than those that the Soviet Union would dare publicly announce for fear of arousing the United States. In a thoroughly un-Marxist maneuver, Mao Tse-tung even exploited the fact that as an Asian he had more appeal to the colored peoples of the world than did the Soviet Union. In practice, if not in theory, Peking exploited the racial issue, even linking the American Negro with other oppressed minorities, in a bid for leadership of the Afro-Asian world. These efforts met with furious opposition on the part of the Soviet Union, which used all its resources of doctrine and money to spoil the Chinese maneuver. By the spring of 1966 the Chinese, in spite of tremendous efforts in Africa, Latin America, and Southeast Asia, suffered many reverses. The Chinese representatives were thrown out of several African states, nor did they fare well in Latin America, especially Cuba. Most disastrous of all was the failure of the September 30 movement in Indonesia, which led to a massive bloodletting at the expense of the Indonesian Communist Party and strained Indonesian relations with Communist China. The Chinese had to accept the failure to achieve victory in Vietnam in 1965 and call the signals for a long and protracted struggle. The successful efforts of Peking to exacerbate relations between Pakistan and India were countered by the unusual peacemaking moves of the Soviet Union, which brought these two countries together in Tashkent and stopped the war. Even the war between Indonesia and Malaysia was ended by the new Indonesian government in the spring of 1966. It looked as if Chinese Communist foreign policy were in a shambles.

It is well to remind ourselves of what might have happened if the Indonesian army had not succeeded in preventing the coup of October 1965. If the Communists had succeeded, it would have been a tremendous victory for Peking, which openly supported the movement, and a disaster for Malaysia and the rest of Southeast Asia. Thailand would have been caught in a pincer movement with Communist forces on either side. The Straits of Malacca would have been under Communist control, and the American position in Vietnam could have been serious indeed. The Indonesian coup was a bold and daring maneuver which cost Peking very little in men and materials. In spite of the damage to Peking's prestige in Indonesia and some of the countries of Africa, the whole effort should not be written off as a total loss. When armies get into control of governments, political power tends to become polarized, and this can be helpful to the Communist movement. Nor does the fact that the Chinese Communists have lost ground in the rivalry with the Soviet Union mean that the world position of the Communist movement, in Latin America especially, has suffered very greatly. Peking's losses are often Moscow's gains.

V

If these are the aims of Communist China, to what extent does she have the capacity to carry them out? There is no easy answer to a question so complex and with so many variables. Much depends upon the relations between Peking and Moscow, the extent to which the Russian nuclear umbrella still covers Peking, the ways in which Moscow will be compelled to support Peking's policies, and the ways in which she will block them. To what extent will the acquisition of a nuclear striking power compensate in prestige for the losses suffered on the economic side as a consequence of the Great Leap Forward, of the communes, the withdrawal of Russian aid, and the concentration of much of the national effort on military power? We are obviously not thinking of China as a great power in any sense of the term except the extent of territory and the number of people. Measured by any other standards, such as per capita production or consumption, gross national product, or military capacity, China is low on the list. By the same token, however, so was the Soviet Union in 1923 when it associated itself with the Chinese Nationalist movement and came near to taking it over. The Chinese-sponsored guerrilla warfare in Malaya took some ten years to suppress. When the political situation is ripe, the thing that counts is the comparatively small material assistance, the moral and political support, and the decisive ingredients of training and revolutionary experience.

The Russians and the Chinese Communists both agree upon the major technique for eroding the power and influence of the Western world. This is the war of national liberation. The war of national liberation has been developed into a highly sophisticated form of struggle that takes in practically every dimension of human life. At a time when proliferation of nuclear weapons makes full-scale war too dangerous to indulge in, the world balance of power can be shifted by successful wars of national liberation.

The nuclear stalemate between the great powers is not necessarily in permanent balance, for the balance does not merely depend on the relative number of missiles available to each side. It is also affected by the control of strategic positions, access to resources and markets, by prestige and credibility, and finally by the will, tenacity, and purpose of the leadership of great states. All these factors can change the situation. There can also be a technological breakthrough or disarmament agreements. One of the main purposes of the wars of national liberation is to bring about these changes. We have just watched the partial failure of the dramatic move to take over Southeast Asia by encirclement — an operation that depended for success upon the seizure of power in Indonesia by the Indonesian Communist Party. If the attempt had succeeded, the loss to the West in terms of economics and strategic positions would have been great indeed. Equally costly would have been the psychological boost that this would have given to the Communist cause in parts of the world close to home.

There are those who have argued that the people's wars are doomed to failure and that wars of national liberation are not for export, that the conditions in the world do not favor them and that we can write off the dangers. This view is superficial and misleading. Wars of national liberation have been proved successful and are still a formidable weapon.

What is a war of national liberation? It is useful to see it from the point of view of those who sponsor such wars. One of the latest Soviet statements on the subject published in *Kommunist,* November 1964, describes modern national liberation revolutions as a product of our time characterized by the transition from capitalism to socialism. They are designed to complete the process of eradicating imperialism. The first stage, the liberation from imperialist political control, has been largely completed, a process for which the Communists claim full credit. But now the liberated colonies must be freed from economic dependence on the Western world and the international capitalist division of labor, and turned to socialism — in other words, be brought within the Communist orbit. So the national liberation revolutions of our time are "anti-imperialist democratic revolutions of a new type." The basic aim, therefore, of the national liberation movement is to move into the next phase, the socialist revolution. This the Communists believe to be possible on a world-wide basis because capitalism is on the decline and cannot "offer an inspiring prospect to the masses in the newly independent countries and mobilize their energies for national reconstruction." Do all the backward countries have to go through capitalism in order to reach socialism? Certainly not. They can bypass capitalism, and the socialist community can help them to do this even if they are geographically remote from it. There can be a variety of transitional forms such as the state of "national democracy." Nor does the political coalition that directs the process of transition to the noncapitalist path of development necessarily have to be headed by a Communist party. In other words, the road followed by China is not the only road. But in many former colonies and semicolonies where the "local bourgeoisie" is weak and the Communist Party is not in a position of leadership, the intermediate sections of the population — peasantry, lower middle classes in the towns, and democratic intelligentsia — gain political independence and play an active role. Their interests are expressed by "revolutionary democrats." It is therefore proper for the Soviet Union to support the "revolutionary democrats" in the newly emerging countries, for example Nehru and Sukarno. "The existence of ideological differences is no obstacle to the joint participation of Communists and revolutionary democrats in the practical implementation of the program of social progress, in the joint struggle for the socialist future of the newly independent countries."

The Soviet statement by implication criticizes the approach advocated by Lin Piao in his well-known statement of September 1965. The Lin Piao, or rather the Maoist, approach is in the Russian view too simplistic. It projects for other countries the experience of the Communist Party in China and ignores the more subtle, long-range type of Soviet aid and assistance to "revolutionary democrats" which may be successful in countries where the Mao approach would be disastrous. As to general strategy, to use the "third world" — Latin America, Africa, Southeast Asia in the main — to change the world balance of forces to the disadvantage of the Western world, there is no disagreement. The real disagreement is on who should guide, lead, control, and get the credit for any successes that might develop.

Such is the ideological foundation for the wars of national liberation. Of equal importance is the carefully developed organizational approach. The general strategy has been laid down by Mao and in the case of Vietnam by General Giap, and most people by now are aware of the three main stages in the development of an insurgency movement to take over the government of other countries. Not everyone is aware, however, of the help that Communist China or the Soviet Union can give to a small country in the way of training cadres, revolutionary experience, political support, and material assistance. Years of patient effort go into the building of organizations among the people and to infiltrating the institutions and armed forces of the other side. Years of patient and arduous labor go into the development of military bases, as in Vietnam. These can be destroyed with superior forces. But the really difficult job is to destroy the Communist political organization. This task can be done, as the French writer Colonel Trinquier has shown us in his book *Modern Warfare: A French View of Counterinsurgency*, if there is sufficient knowledge and understanding of the enemy and adequate resolution and force to finish the task. It is not easy to stop a war of national liberation, because most of the war is over before large-scale fighting begins. The war has taken place on the organizational front, largely in secret.

A good case can be made that the balance of world forces might very well be shifted seriously against the West if a significant portion of the "third world" were brought under Communist control. The question is whether it can be done. Everyone admits that the Maoist formula worked quite well for a time in the Philippines and Malaya and has gone a long way in Vietnam. It did quite well in Cuba. If present trends continue, one can also argue that there will be plenty of raw material in the way of social tensions and human misery for the Communist cadres to work with. The World Bank list of developing countries, for example, includes all of Latin America, Africa except for South Africa, Asia except for Japan, and Turkey, Greece, Albania, Yugoslavia, Spain, and Portugal: about 70 per cent of the people of the world. The prospects for economic growth in this part of the world are not encouraging. The total gross national product for this group of countries was $170 billion in 1960 and $200 billion in 1964, whereas the gross national product of the developed countries — United States, Canada, Japan, and the industrialized countries of Western Europe — rose from $920 billion in 1960 to $1,100 billion in 1964. The international capitalist division of labor, as the Communists would put it, means that the rich countries are getting richer and the poorer countries, relatively poorer. The developing countries send 75 per cent of their exports to the developed countries and borrow from them practically all the capital they use. Their problem is to make enough from these exports to provide the capital they need for internal development at a time when prices of raw materials, always subject to serious fluctuations, are tending to go down while the prices of manufactured goods are going up. The earnings from exports therefore are not going up rapidly enough to sustain an adequate growth rate, and in most of these countries the living standards are stationary. The increase in national income barely keeps up with the growth of population. As the level of development assistance to the developing countries has been stationary now for some time, we can anticipate that the living standards of most of the "third world" will not improve for the rest of this century.

Of particular interest to Peking is the fact that the economic growth in the developing countries has been much greater in manufacturing and mining than in agriculture. This part of the world in general is not growing enough food to keep pace with increasing population and the rise in standards of consumption. The developing countries, whose economy is mainly agricultural, are food-deficit areas. Food imports run around four billion dollars a year, plus about one billion dollars' worth under U.S. Public Law 480. The toughest part of the problem of development, perhaps, is the difficulty of changing social relations in the villages of the "third world" in such a way as to make possible a rapid rise in agricultural productivity, an essential condition to other advances in the economy. To increase production, both per capita and per acre, the farmer must use machines and science. The experience of Japan, the only Asian country, except for Taiwan, to break out of the vicious circle of rural poverty, shows that this calls for land reform and sweeping institutional and social changes. Merely to reduce population growth is not the answer, for under most Asian farming conditions to reduce the human capital investment on the land is merely to reduce production. Nor has the farmer any economic incentives to reduce the size of his family when human hands are the only capital he possesses. The bare facts are that even if the governments of the "third world" were all able, determined, and dedicated to the improvement of the lot of the people, and even if the Western world were ready to throw all necessary resources behind their efforts, it would still be an extremely slow process to improve the economy.

The political significance of all this is that Peking can probably count, certainly for the next ten or twenty years, upon a tremendous amount of human misery, frustration, and impoverishment in the "third world." This does not mean that the wars of national liberation will necessarily find fertile soil; many other factors are involved. The fact that the poor will remain relatively poor does not necessarily mean that they will be easy to organize in wars of national liberation. According to the economists of the World Bank, we should engage in a "development war" and should begin by making available to the poor countries foreign exchange in the amount of four to five billion dollars more than we do now. Those in the developed countries who are frustrated and disillusioned with the results of foreign aid so far do not always realize that the leaders and aspiring leaders in the developing countries are even more impatient and frustrated when they consider the enormity of their problems. Even more than the poverty itself, it is the frustration of those who lead or aspire to leadership in the developing countries that provides the combustible material for the making of wars of national liberation.

VI

The policy of Communist China has serious implications for American policy. It is clear that Communist China is a global as well as a regional problem. Its resources are limited, but they are adequate for the type of warfare in which she specializes, and she still draws additional influence in world affairs from the general world position of the Communist bloc. Communist China is aided in her ambition to wield more influence in the world by the weapons changes since World War II that have practically outlawed unlimited war between states. She was also assisted by economic trends that divide the developed and the developing countries. The struggle with the Soviet Union is costly and debilitating, but it is a necessary basis for the establishment of Chinese Communist leadership in Asia, and it makes Peking's appeal to traditional Chinese nationalism all the more credible. At the same time it keeps alive a competitive aggressiveness between the two biggest Communist countries and contributes an unpredictable and irrational factor in world politics. There seems to be no reason to expect any change, certainly in the immediate future, in the policy objectives of Communist China. Changes can be expected only in tactics, which in the past have varied all the way from the Bandung spirit to the invasion of India.

The United States policy since the Korean War has been to make arrangements for the military containment of Communist China, but this was only a special aspect of the more general policy of seeking to preserve the political independence of small powers and to underwrite their independence by the offer of technical aid and economic assistance and, where acceptable, military aid. Largely as the result of the Korean conflict, the United States does not recognize Communist China, does not trade with her, and has blocked any moves in the United Nations to accept the credentials of Peking. Communist China's acquisition of a nuclear capability, and her role in the Vietnamese war, have to be considered in the constant review of our policies. There is no reason to change the general thrust of our policy, but there is good reason to devise ways and means of meeting the challenge where it is most dangerous, in the "third world," and to find the answer to the war of national liberation and other forms of Communist-style imperialism.

U.S.-SOVIET DÉTENTE?

MARSHALL SHULMAN

For those who like their politics simple, with one map color for friends and another for enemies, the present tide of international politics is running in the wrong direction. After a decade or two of sharp polarities, we find ourselves in a fog of ambiguities. The lines that once sharply defined allegiances are blurred. The confrontation of blocs is not past, but in some undefined way, it has changed. Alliances are marbled by the surfacing of long-repressed conflicts, and enmities are tempered by a growing awareness of some common concerns. The level of tension is neither crackling with imminent alarms, nor euphoric, but in some absent-minded middle ground.

Whatever may have been the real conflicts of interest which powered the cold war — and it remains for historians to disentangle the political and psychological interactions of the postwar period with the detachment that is becoming now more possible — we find ourselves in need of some fresh conceptual tools to deal with the mixture of conflict and overlapping interests which has come to characterize the present relationship between the United States and the Soviet Union.

To reduce the risk of being misunderstood, it must be said at the very outset that this does not mean swinging from one extreme to another on a simple scale between friendship and hostility. What it does mean is a search for a way of describing a relationship in which elements of conflict and elements of some common interests are intermixed in an undefined and changing balance.

The question asked by the title of this chapter has led to some confusing discussion in the past, partly because the word "détente" has been the source of much misunderstanding. Unfortunately, we do not have words to distinguish between a relaxation in the climate of tension and a substantive improvement of relations. As a result, it often happens that actions on the atmospheric plane of international relations are taken as a symbol that changes have taken place at a more substantial level — even a reversal of alliances, according to the hopes of some and the fears of others. In this sense, the word "détente" is quite often confused with another French contribution to the language of diplomacy — "rapprochement" — and also with the imprecise Soviet term, "peaceful coexistence."

To avoid these confusions, let us be clear that what we are talking about in this chapter goes beyond the tactical or the atmospheric sense of the question. On that plane, we recognize that the climate at the moment of writing is neither one of extreme tension nor of close cooperation; it might be described as a climate of "limited détente," subject to tactical fluctations in response to such factors as the Sino-Soviet dispute, the war in Vietnam, domestic, political and economic preoccupations, and so on. But at a more fundamental level, what we are concerned with is the longer-term evolutionary process which has brought the Soviet Union and the United States into what can perhaps best be described as a "limited adversary relationship." Perhaps in time a less cumbersome nomenclature may emerge to describe this relationship. Such terms as "rivalry" or "competition" have been suggested, but these may still be premature for the residual conflict of political expectations. It is indeed a delicate and difficult question of political judgment to say just how operative the ideological component of Soviet foreign policy may be at any one time, or in regard to any particular issue, for the mode by which this evolution is taking place is through the elongation of its time perspectives. The more distant the period in which the ultimate goals of Communist ideology are expected to be realized, the more traditional nation-state interests tend to be the actual determinants of foreign policy actions in the present. But this evolution does not take place uniformly; certain areas of foreign policy, especially those concerned with the relations among the Communist-bloc countries, are charged with a higher degree of ideological intensity than others. What may be said for the present is that, while the ultimate political expectations of the Soviet Union and the United States seem irreconcilable, the ultimate is a long way off and receding into the future, while the immediate landscape is crowded with problems demanding practical adjustments.

What the term "limited adversary relationship" is intended to suggest is a condition in which the emphasis may be at one time upon the "adversary" aspect of the relationship, and at another time upon the limits within which this hostility operates. What we have witnessed over the past fifteen or perhaps twenty years has been a learning process, through which the United States and the Soviet Union have become aware, in the course of crises and aborted crises, of the limits which self-interest imposes on their conflict with each other. The result has been the development in practice of a number of tacit restraints, which begin in the military realm, and have been extending into the political field.

I

It may seem a paradox that the qualitative change in military technology has been an important factor in encouraging this evolution. At the dawn of the nuclear weapons age, there were many dire predictions that nations would have to accept an international authority, or that an unbridled arms race would lead inexorably toward cataclysm. It may be too soon for self-congratulation, but what appears to have happened is that the arms race has shown certain self-limiting qualities, even in the absence of formal international agreements. The condition of mutual deterrence, which allows for a gross equilibrium even in the presence of substantial inequalities among the great powers, has given rise to a partial stabilization in the strategic weapons field. The question whether this stabilization is a temporary or an enduring condition is one to which we will turn in a few moments. In recent years, at any rate, the arms race has not been proceeding at anything like an all-out pace, and restraints in procurement and deployment of weapons have reflected a growing awareness of the interacting effects of each side's efforts to improve its own power position. It is by now fairly well accepted that optimum security, which is still a very relative term, is not to be equated with maximum quantitative superiority in weapons, but also must take account of the qualitative condition of stability of the military confrontation as a whole. We should not minimize the importance of the restraints that have flowed from this awareness for the reason that they have been tacit rather than embodied in formal agreements.

Perhaps it will seem to some to be another paradox that it is not only the partial stabilization based upon the condition of mutual deterrence which creates a certain easement of tension, but the realization by the great powers of the limited usefulness of strategic nuclear weapons. Ever since Korea, the great powers have found themselves preoccupied with a range of problems for which strategic nuclear weapons were either inapplicable, or, at best, only indirectly useful. This refers not only to limited war situations, but also to conflicts of an essentially political or economic character, where resources, organizational energy, diplomatic skill, or the mobilization of ideas may be more effective forms of power than nuclear missiles. Here too a process of learning has been at work, as the political consequences of the nuclear age have gradually been unfolding. While in times of tension and crisis, the fundamental configuration of power is still bipolar, the easement of tension flowing from the partial stabilization in the strategic field gives rein to multiple forms of power from many sources, and releases medium and smaller nations to follow policies of greater flexibility and independence.

The net effect of this development has been to create certain parallelisms within the Communist and the non-Communist world, and even certain parallel interests on the part of the Soviet Union and the United States. It may be well to speak of these as parallel rather than common interests, since they may involve actions of tacit collaboration for somewhat different reasons, as in the case of the Tashkent negotiations. In its broadest terms, the dominant external concerns of the two superpowers in the present period are not with each other, but with the political forces released by various forms of nationalism in other parts of the world. While each side seeks to turn these forces to its own advantage, neither power could benefit from the outbreak of violence as the result of the clash of these political forces. Thus, such issues as third-area turbulence or the spread of nuclear weapons are threatening to both superpowers, and within limits are subject to the possibility of some collaborative or parallel action. Of course the rise of Communist China as a power and its exacerbating role in these local conflict situations has been an important factor in this development, although its challenge to Soviet orthodoxy and militancy has inhibited Soviet recognition of these possibilities for parallel action.

II

We come now to some questions about predictions and policy choices. Is this degree of recognition of limited parallelism of interest on its way toward becoming a more substantial collaboration, or is it a temporary lull in the conflict? What factors govern its evolution? And to the extent that we can influence this process, in what direction should we seek to do so?

Over the long run, the most important factors governing this relationship are probably those external to either country. Changes in the leadership and politics within these countries may be of decisive importance at any one moment, but it is the condition of the environment of international politics which creates the underlying imperatives to which both nations, sooner or later, by one means or another, are obliged to respond.

Among these external factors, one which seems likely to exert an important influence on the future course of U.S.-Soviet relations is the prospect for continued turbulence and upheaval in the underdeveloped areas of the world. Although the Vietnam war has many unique aspects, in a broad sense it represents a class of conflicts which may dominate the coming period in international politics. The seeds of these conflicts are to be found in many forms all over Africa, Asia, and Latin America: religious and tribal conflicts, competition between rival leadership groups, boundary disputes, color, race, and above all, the frustrations of modernization and nation-building in an environment of poverty and illiteracy. Advances in the technology of transportation and communications have made it virtually impossible for any local conflict to avoid becoming entangled in global complications. In most areas of potential violence, the great-power involvement is triangular, involving the United States, the Soviet Union, and Communist China. The present policy of Communist China, which seeks to radicalize and exacerbate local protest movements as part of a broad "anti-imperialist" strategy, sees the increase of its influence in maximizing conflict, particularly between the other two powers. Soviet policy seeks to balance its rivalry with China in various areas as against its striving for competitive advantage against the United States. For its part, the United States appears to be evolving a strategy which combines in some indeterminate degree an interest in the status quo, or some conception of development in an environment of stability, with its competition with the Soviet Union and the military and political containment of China.

Within this critical triangular confrontation, the most likely variables, leaving aside a possible sea change in Chinese policy, are two: alternations in the Soviet strategy vis-à-vis China; and a further development in the Soviet definition of its interests in relation to local conflict situations. These are obviously interrelated, for a decision by the Soviet leadership to make more strenuous use of the peace issue in the Sino-Soviet dispute, as it did in 1963 at the time of the signing of the partial test ban, instead of proving by verbal militancy that it was not guilty of collaboration with the imperialists or of lack of revolutionary ardor, would also increase its freedom of maneuver in response to local conflict situations. Here a range of possible lines of action are open for future diplomatic exploration, from unilateral peacemaking (on the model of Tashkent), through *ad hoc* agreements with the United States to limit the flow of weapons into an area (such as the Middle East), to the wider acceptance of United Nations mechanisms for peaceful settlement and peace-keeping. Perhaps there is a spectrum among local conflict situations, from those in which the conflicting political expectations of the United States and the Soviet Union are too strong to permit either explicit or even tacit collaboration, extending at the other end of the spectrum to those in which the risks or disadvantages of potential violence may be greater than any hope of political gain by either side. The Middle East and the Indo–Pakistani relationship may be examples of conflicts at this latter end of the spectrum, offering the most favorable possibilities for common or parallel action.

Another external factor which affects the environment of international politics and thereby influences the character of the U.S.-Soviet relationship is the phenomenon of the rising nationalism which is manifesting itself in a variety of forms in both the underdeveloped and the industrialized parts of the world in the present period. Perhaps the term "nationalism" is too undiscriminating for the various expressions of this surge of political energy, which provides the dynamism for nation-building among the new nations, and expresses itself in a thrust for greater self-reliance or independence of action among the relatively industrialized allies of the United States and the Soviet Union. In a more analytical context, these manifestations would obviously require more differentiated treatment, but for our present purposes it may suffice to observe that the driving force of national identity has once again become the most potent source of political energy on the international scene, and is a major factor in the fragmentation of the power bloc alliances which formerly defined the configuration of international politics. Whether this is a cyclical phenomenon, reappearing after a period of suppression in the aftermath of World War II, or whether it is unloosed by the relaxation of tension, the growth of economic power in Western Europe and Japan, the abrupt liquidation of colonial relationships, and other specific factors, remains as yet unclear, but the consequence of this development is to require of both the Soviet Union and the United States a recalculation of their respective political strategies.

From the point of view of the United States, the most immediately serious effect of this resurgent nationalism has been felt in Western Europe, where Gaullism is the most dramatic but by no means the sole expression of this political current. It is still difficult to say whether the nascent process of European integration has now been diverted for a period into a phase of intensified chauvinism, and whether the "European movement," instead of defining itself as a stage in the evolution toward some form of Atlanticism, now draws its force from a continental chauvinism, finding its identity in opposition to the influence of the United States. Obviously, the emergence of Europe, or at least of Western Europe, as a somewhat separate power center, at least in the political and economic realm in the first instance, creates a new political setting for the U.S.-Soviet confrontation. For the United States, the question posed is whether it is capable of defining a more resilient relationship, capable of giving expression to the European desire for a separate identity, within a framework of a common strategic defense and some coordination of political and economic policies. For the Soviet Union, the question posed is how far it can, or would wish to, take advantage of divisive strains within the Western alliance: to what extent it would benefit from a total removal of U.S. power and influence from the European continent; what political forces would then be dominant on the continent; and whether the net effect would be more favorable or more hazardous to Soviet interests.

For many years, Soviet policy has made use of nationalist appeals outside its own sphere, particularly as a counter to the U.S. influence in Western Europe, but it has made strenuous efforts to extirpate the same force within its own sphere of influence and control. Now, with the intensification of nationalism in Eastern as well as Western Europe, the disintegrative effects of this force have been obliging the Soviet Union to seek some more resilient form of relationship with the states of Eastern Europe, and the institutions of the Warsaw Pact and Comecon, the Council for Mutual Economic Assistance, are in the process of continuous adjustment and redefinition of authority and function.

A concomitant effect of the trends sketched in the previous paragraphs has been a new sense of fluidity in the relations between Eastern and Western Europe. This fluidity has multiple effects.

One effect stems from the fact that the current impelling East and West Europe toward each other draws its force from popular feelings on both sides, to such a degree that it is partly independent of direction by the major powers. This is seen in the manifold, semiautonomous efforts to establish lines of contact, particularly in trade and cultural affairs. To some extent, this impulsion operates beneath the surface, relatively free from the vicissitudes which raise and lower the level of the détente between the Soviet Union and the United States, although in the first instance, this trend originated in the permissive atmosphere of the early détente.

Another effect has been to change the rules of the political contest between the great powers in Europe. It has by now been fairly well accepted that each side is reasonably free to maneuver for advantage within the other's sphere of influence, within limits. The United States accepts without violent reaction the increasing trade and cultural presence of the Soviet Union in Western Europe, and demurs in modulated tones against Soviet efforts to manipulate the political orientation of Paris, Bonn, or London. Similarly, the old arguments about "roll-back" or "liberation" have given way to accepted efforts by the United States to encourage an increased degree of autonomy by the states of Eastern Europe, it being understood that fundamental security interests of the Soviet Union are not being challenged.

A related effect concerns the increased discussion in the recent period concerning the future of Germany and the possibility of some kind of a European settlement. In part this is a response to the rise of the reunification issue in West German domestic politics, but so far at least the discussion has not approached serious negotiating possibilities, largely because of the difficulty of reconciling German reunification with the Soviet reliance upon its position in the Eastern zone, or with the Federal Republic's attachment to the Western alliance. Meanwhile, however, the issue continues to be agitated in terms of various procedural suggestions, to gain relative advantage on the propaganda plane of politics. The issue is complicated by the continuing focus of Soviet intensive propaganda attacks on the themes of "militarism" and "revanchism" in the Federal Republic. While it is understandable that Soviet memories of the past and apprehensions for the future should lead to a deeply felt preoccupation with militarism in Germany, it is a serious question whether the very lack of discrimination in these broadside attacks serves Soviet long-term interests. The Soviet Union, as much as the rest of the world, has an interest in the evolution of the political life of Germany, and it is doubtful whether the short-term advantages to the Soviet Union of manipulating the "revanchist" theme in an undiscriminating way is worth the cost over the long run in inhibiting the emergence of a healthy, peaceful, democratic (in the true sense of the word) political leadership group in Germany. Nor is this tactic useful as a counter to the economic strength of the Federal Republic; the effect of the endless repetition of the "revanchist" and "militarist" slogans is to give encouragement to potential demagogic exploitation of nationalist themes, feeding on isolation and resentment, and to direct Germany's growing economic strength toward unconstructive uses. A larger view of Soviet long-term interests would suggest that one of the areas of overlapping interests with the United States is precisely here, in creating an environment favorable to the evolution of a responsible and peaceful Germany, which can find room for its fulfillment within the framework of a European and world community.

Another closely related effect of the pan-European fluidity has been the revival of various plans for arms control in Europe. A spate of new and revised proposals for forms of disengagement, demilitarization, or denuclearization have made their reappearance, but the context has changed from the 1950's, when such plans had a certain vogue. At that time, the major concern which prompted these plans was the fear of surprise attack, or the fear that friction between the major powers at their points of peripheral contact might lead to war. Now, however, the change in the character of strategic weapons systems has reduced the fear of surprise attack as an inauguration of central war, and the growth of restraint and responsibility among the major powers has raised a question whether the contact of their forces in Europe may not create relatively more stability than if they were absent, at least while Germany remains divided. Therefore, the emphasis in the current discussion of plans for military stabilization in Europe tends to be upon other considerations, including: reduction of the financial costs and the manpower drain of maintaining large forces in East and West Europe; promoting the autonomy of the Eastern European states by reducing Soviet forces in the area;

adjusting potential crisis points, such as the Western access to Berlin; and inhibiting the flow of nuclear weapons into the area.

It is clear that the level of anxiety about the possibility of war in Europe is sufficiently lowered so that there is not a compelling pressure from an arms-control point of view for a search in this direction; rather the impulsion comes from hopes for some form of political evolution. There is no doubt that an agreement of any sort in this area would have a powerful symbolic effect supporting a climate of détente, but so long as the problem of Germany remains outside any overlapping negotiating positions, it is difficult to see how any significant agreement on arms control in Central Europe can be achieved. It is quite possible, however, that budgetary pressures upon the major powers may result in some force reductions in Europe, but this would be likely to be the result, rather than the cause, of continued low tensions.

Before concluding this section of the discussion on the effect of a resurgent nationalism upon the U.S.-Soviet relationship, it is worth recalling that nationalism has been traditionally antipathetic to the appeals of "Communist internationalism," and continues to represent a particular obstacle for a political philosophy which is committed to a process of social change toward some unified international conception, however remote. This is seen not only in pressures toward the emergence of forms of "national communism," but also in the persistence of the nationalist character of revolutionary movements in the underdeveloped areas. With the possible exception of the Communist movement of North Vietnam, there has not been a successful fusion of nationalist and Communist revolutionary leaderships in the former colonial and other areas of Asia, Africa, and Latin America. This fact has been an important consideration in the evolution of Soviet policy toward the underdeveloped areas, leading toward a gradual acceptance of the necessity for dealing with nationalist leaderships on the basis of traditional power politics, and the continued postponement of social and political revolution, at least for the intermediate term. This evolution in turn has been an important factor contributing to the possibility of parallel or collaborative action by the Soviet Union and the United States in parts of the underdeveloped world.

A third factor in the external environment governing the U.S. Soviet relationship and the future prospects of the détente is the further development of military technology. There is some complacency on this score, possibly because we appear to have been on a relative plateau of military scientific discoveries, compared to the late war and immediate postwar years, and also because the technological contributions over the past decade, such as the development of missile delivery systems, have in the main contributed to military stability. But it is by no means assured that future military technological developments will automatically strengthen the present degree of partial stabilization in the strategic weapons field.

While the present intensive concentration of research and development energies upon antimissile capabilities does not yet appear to have made feasible a system capable of protecting urban areas from a large-scale attack, enough progress has been made to raise the question whether the deployment of even rudimentary missile defense systems around Soviet and United States urban areas would be useful. If this were to be done on any substantial scale, it is likely that a new spiral in the arms race would result, for the riposte to an adversary's missile defense system is not only to match it by corresponding action, but also to counter it by an increase in offensive power. Since these systems are enormously costly, the effect would be a great increase in military budgets, a stimulation of research and development of offensive weapons, and a large-scale involvement in civil-defense measures as a necessary support for urban missile defense installations.

Under these conditions, the political and psychological climate would certainly reflect a considerable increase in tension, whether or not the missile defense systems themselves were thought to have a technically destabilizing effect. The question is complicated by the existence of other nuclear powers, for a Soviet antimissile defense system might seem more credible against French capabilities than against American; and a United States antimissile defense is sometimes advocated against potential Chinese capabilities. But it would be difficult to insulate such systems from effectively setting the great powers into a new effort against each other, or from creating a demand from allied countries for help in installing comparable antimissile protective systems. The result would be the acquisition of a capability of dubious military value at a considerable political price, and a net decrease in security on all sides.

This is an instance, therefore, of technological change which could have the effect of unsettling the present partial stabilization in the strategic weapons field, and of creating an increase in international tension, unless it is consciously restrained by the great powers. Another instance may be cited as illustrative of this category: the prospect of simpler and cheaper methods for the production of fissionable materials, and the consequent facilitation of the further spread of nuclear weapons. While modern weapons systems have grown more sophisticated and more expensive, and the capability of waging a general nuclear war is likely to remain limited to capability of the two great powers, it is also the case that *some* military nuclear capability will be within the reach of a larger number of middle powers, and even of the smaller powers, if one allows for the possibility of transfer of weapons. As of this writing, the Soviet Union and the United States have been prevented by a senseless wrangle on Germany from acting upon what is surely a common interest in preventing the further spread of nuclear weapons. If they are unable to resolve this difficulty, the resulting increase in the number of military nuclear powers will probably make the maintenance of the present degree of détente more complicated, and may greatly increase the hazard of enlargement of local conflicts. If, on the other hand, the Soviet Union and the United States are able to agree upon a nonproliferation treaty and take other measures required to inhibit the spread of nuclear weapons, the effect of this agreement would be generally felt in the reduction of international tension, as well as specifically useful in translating a common interest into common action.

III

We turn now from these factors in the general political environment to examine the place of détente in the political strategies of the Soviet Union and the United States. Here we become aware at once what a catch-all the term détente is, and how much more precision is required to deal with the mixture of considerations entering into the explicit policy choices confronting the two great powers in their relations with each other. Rarely is the choice cast in terms of a preference for high versus low tensions; rather, what is involved is an assignment of priorities as between conflicting considerations, and the result dictates what inflection of the détente is required by current political strategy.

In the case of the Soviet Union, the political strategy defined as "peaceful coexistence" is broad enough to encompass widely varying levels of tension, and a differentiation of tensions as between one area and another. In practice, détente may imply any degree of substantiality from the plane of atmospherics to specific agreements, either across the board, or selectively applied to various countries.

The weight of Soviet experience in recent years has tended to favor a policy of operating at minimum levels of tension, within the limits of the situation at hand. Both domestic and foreign policy considerations have encouraged the evolution of Soviet policy in this direction.

In the past, domestic political considerations occasionally dictated the generation of external hostilities, but it is undoubtedly the case today both in the Soviet Union and in Eastern Europe that the mobilization of popular support for a political leadership can be accomplished more effectively by the peace issue than by the manipulation of controls under the shadow of foreign threats. The concentration of energies upon the repair of domestic economic shortcomings, the reduction of military costs, and the improvement of foreign trade prospects are all considerations which argue for policies of minimum tensions.

On the foreign policy side, high tensions in the past have had the effect of mobilizing the Western alliance, stimulating U.S. military expenditures, and encouraging the cohesion of the West under American leadership. Conversely, periods of reduced tension have encouraged fragmentation within the Western alliance, and reduced American military and foreign aid expenditures.

Within the international Communist movement, while periods of low tension and political collaboration have created difficulties for the militant cadres in certain areas, they have created opportunities for mass political action on the part of the large Communist parties of Western Europe.

However, in the recent period, two factors have introduced conflicting considerations: the war in Vietnam, and the Sino-Soviet dispute. In a measured degree, the Soviet leadership has sought to bring pressure against the United States action in Vietnam by generalizing the tension to the entire range of relations. This action has been heightened by Soviet sensitivity to Chinese Communist charges that the Soviet leadership has lost revolutionary ardor, and has engaged in collusion with the "American imperialists." The consequence has been an avoidance of any appearance of bilateral cooperation in all fields, and a campaign of domestic and Eastern European propaganda against the United States in a restrained middle range of hostility. Concurrently, the Soviet Union has shown a receptivity for improved relations with other industrial countries of the West, except for the Federal Republic of Germany, which continues to be a major propaganda target.

This differentiated détente enables Soviet policy to take advantage of divisive trends within the Western alliance; for example, to exploit possibilities for a pan-European conference without the United States, to improve trade and cultural relations with France, Canada, Japan, and India, and to inflect relations with England according to its policies toward the Vietnam war.

While there are undoubtedly some tactical advantages in this Soviet policy of limited or differentiated détente, there is at least room for questioning whether on balance this policy serves Soviet long-term interests as well as would a policy which sought for more substantive collaboration with the United States. Briefly stated, here are some of the questions which must be taken into account:

1) Are such general forms of pressure as the cancellation of sports and cultural contacts likely to be as effective in influencing U.S. policy in Vietnam as a collaborative effort to induce negotiations?

2) Is a militant Soviet response to the Chinese Communist charges as effective in maintaining leadership of the world Communist movement as one which dramatized the Soviet championing of peace?

3) Would the elimination of United States influence from Western Europe be a salutary development from the Soviet point of view?

4) Does the indefinite postponement of substantial progress toward reducing the risks of general war, inhibiting the proliferation of nuclear weapons, moderating the arms race, and collaborative efforts in dealing with third-area conflicts, genuinely serve Soviet long-term interests?

If, as is implied, there is some merit in a negative answer to these questions, perhaps subsequent reassessments will argue for a policy which seeks to implement the détente in more general and more substantive terms.

Of course such a reassessment would require that reciprocal developments would have to take place in United States policy, which also can be seen as a resultant in a process of assigning priorities as between conflicting considerations.

The principal inhibitions which limit American acceptance of a détente policy differ according to the various senses of the word "détente." In its most substantial sense, the idea of a détente appears to be in conflict with United States alliance interests. In particular, the fear of a rapprochement between the Soviet Union and the United States has flared up in Western European capitals on very slight provocation, reflecting an anxiety that the interests of Western European nations might be compromised in a great-power deal. Recent trends, however, have been toward acceptance of the idea that the interests of West European nations are better served by a low-tension relationship between the great powers than the converse. Since the present looser structure of the Western alliance is in large measure a product of a reduced perception of threat from the Soviet Union, and since both France and England have been in advance of the United States in exploring the possibilities of a détente, the remaining essential question concerns the confidence of the Federal Republic of Germany that the United States commitment to the principle of the future reunification of Germany will not be weakened in a détente situation. This confidence, which is an important factor in the stability and responsibility of the political life of the Federal Republic, is therefore a vital consideration for United States policy.

In the less substantial uses of "détente," to refer to atmospheric measures of tension reduction, there is a suspicion against the manipulative use of this tactic to disarm a volatile public opinion in the West, and in particular in the United States, without any genuine improvement in the situation warranting a reduction in security efforts.

At another level, there is a question of policy which is sometimes raised in Western discussions, whether a reduction of Western military strength in response to a détente situation might not be less conducive to the further modification of Soviet policy in the direction of restraint and responsibility. In its extreme form, the argument is sometimes made that a high level of tension and consequently of military expenditures would, given the comparative economic advantages of the United States, tend to encourage Soviet interest in international agreements for the reduction of armaments. This is not a dominant view in the United States, but the question has been at least in the background of policy debates on this issue.

Here too, as in the case of the Soviet Union, questions can be raised whether apparent short-term advantages may not have to be weighed against longer-term interests. Would it not be shortsighted as well as fruitless to try to re-create the fears of the early cold war period in an effort to maintain the Western alliance on the basis of its original motivation? Can the United States muster the statesmanship to maintain its close association with the nations of Western Europe as a force for stability in the world, on the basis of a realistic assessment of common security interests and of common interests in strengthening progress toward international order? Are not the prospects for German reunification, and for settlement of European problems generally, better served by an evolutionary process under conditions of reduced tension? Are not those evolutionary trends within the Communist world, which are desired by its people and legitimately encouraged by its neighbors, more likely under conditions of reduced tension? Should not the objective of inhibiting the proliferation of nuclear weapons, moderating the arms race; and reducing the violence of third-area conflicts claim the highest priority in United States policy?

Of course when such propositions are couched in these general terms they easily win assent, but their concrete realization in policy terms is infinitely difficult. The real complexities of the problems are obscured when they are discussed in terms of whether or not a détente in a substantial sense is desirable or not. To be realistic, no one can expect that the conflicting philosophies and expectations of the great powers will be talked away, or that policy makers can act as though these conflicts did not exist.

But it is not beyond the bounds of realism to expect that the leaders of the great powers, conscious that the longer-term interests of their respective societies require an enlargement of the area of collaboration, may find it eminently practical to adjust their list of priorities with this objective in mind.

MOSCOW-PEKING RELATIONS IN PERSPECTIVE

RODGER SWEARINGEN

The Communist theory of international relations teaches that world problems, international tensions, disagreements between nations, indeed, even war itself, are all the unfortunate consequences of the presence on this earth of "advanced capitalist countries." Imperialism, we are reminded by Lenin and his followers, is the "final stage of capitalism." As the Communists see it, the solution to the world's ills is obvious: Once all nations have been converted to the socialist, i.e., the Soviet, system, "fraternal peace" will reign, relations between states will become cordial, and prosperity, Communist-style, will be just around the corner.

Serious non-Communist students of Marxism-Leninism have always found this simple, single factor analysis of the world's affairs highly dubious and a quite inadequate explanation of the complicated interrelationships which govern nations and peoples.

By present-day jet-nuclear-space standards the real world of the interwar period, i.e., between World War I and World War II, was a relatively simple world. To the policy planners in Moscow it was even simpler: The prewar globe, as the Communists viewed it, was divided into three parts: The socialist world (then only one country, Soviet Russia), the capitalist world (the industrialized nations of Europe, the United States, Japan, etc.), and the colonial and semicolonial areas (all the other areas of Asia, Africa, the Middle East, and Latin America).

This convenient pattern articulated by Lenin served as the basis for the Kremlin's world-wide Communist strategy for nearly three decades. While prewar Communist policy differed drastically depending on the particular historical period and problems of the moment, the central objective remained clear and well understood by the faithful. It was the conversion of capitalist and colonial or semicolonial states and areas into Moscow-oriented socialist states to be run by the local Communist party.

Polycentrism is the latest term used by the objective analysts to suggest that all this has changed; that there are now at least two Romes; that the classic, monolithic structure of international communism has cracked, perhaps beyond repair. The fact is that international communism has never been unified or completely coordinated — not to say monolithic. From the beginning, Moscow insisted upon calling the tune, even though Trotskyism, Bukharinism, and Li Li-sanism (to name but three deviates) have all challenged "orthodoxy" and at times threatened to destroy the world-wide Communist movement.

What separates the Communist world of today, then, from the pattern of the 1920's and the 1930's is the question of power. What Tito and Mao possess that Bukharin and Li Li-san, and even Trotsky, lacked is a territorial base of operations and absolute control of a national army and a population. "National communism" may have international ambitions (China is a case in point), but it clearly feeds on nationalism and thirsts for national power and prestige quite as much as, or more than, for the unity of the workers of the world.

The record of the Chinese Communists' ties with Moscow is a long one and complicated beyond the scope of this brief consideration. Although the Chinese Communist Party remained as an official branch of the Comintern (the general staff of world communism with headquarters in Moscow), retained representatives in the U.S.S.R., and maintained contact with Soviet leaders, it is clear that, throughout its history, the Chinese leadership reserved for itself wide independence on theory and practice. Three or four points may be worth noting because they condition attitudes and suggest nuances in the present situation. First, the Chinese Communist Party was established in 1921 under the guidance of the Kremlin-controlled Comintern. Comintern personnel, Comintern policy guidance, and Comintern funds were all instrumental in creating the early Party. Second, the Party at its second congress officially joined the Comintern as one of its branches, a relationship which it maintained despite disagreements. Third, at several periods throughout contemporary history, Soviet assistance to the Chinese Communists has been important. Noteworthy in this respect are the years 1924–1927, when Soviet political and military advisers to the nationalist revolutionary government in south China used their position to advance communism in China. Similarly, during the immediate postwar years, 1945–1947, Soviet military forces in Manchuria assisted the Chinese Communists in Yenan by turning over to the Chinese Red Army — or allowing to fall into Chinese Communist hands — millions of items of captured Japanese weapons and equipment.

At the same time a fourth factor must be added to balance the picture: After 1927 Mao Tse-tung adopted policies and programs that were quite different from those put forward by Moscow.

The relatively simple world of the 1920's, 1930's, and early 1940's, as the Communists had conceived it, began to disappear toward the end of World War II. To the original three Marxist-Leninist classifications (socialist, capitalist, colonial-semicolonial) the Kremlin found it necessary to add (1) occupied areas

(Japan, Germany, etc.) and (2) new nations of Asia, Africa, and the Middle East (neither capitalist nor colonial). The stereotyped prewar pattern was further altered by the Soviet "annexation" of Eastern Europe. This changed the foreign affairs picture radically.

The first practical test of the always doubtful Communist theory of international relations came in 1948 when Yugoslavia, a socialist country, broke with Moscow. Impossible! A "socialist" nation, yet anti-Soviet? The faithful in Moscow and abroad were quick to explain the event as resulting from the misguided mentality of a madman, Tito. The sacred Communist assumptions on the nature of foreign relations, if slightly shaken, were not to be abandoned merely due to one "freak accident of history."

By October 1949, a Communist regime was in power in China. A second, major Communist power center — in Asia — had emerged. This event drastically altered the rules of the game, and cast further demonstrable doubt on the Soviet theory of international relations. Those who like to reconstruct the evidence of early Soviet and Comintern political and military aid can produce impressive documentation, some of it noted above, establishing the Chinese Communists' close and consistent ties with Moscow. Others who insist that Mao Tse-tung and company were at times quite independent and on their own resources for much of the critical period of the late 1930's and 1940's can also marshal considerable and convincing evidence. And those others who insist on pinning the blame for the Communist take-over of China on the inadequacies of Chiang Kai-shek or the shortsightedness of U.S. policy can also make a case of sorts.

The pertinent point to the subject at hand is that Communist China came on the world scene with acknowledged, close, and formal ties with Moscow. Mao called the relationship "leaning to one side," the Soviet side. Soviet economic and military aid, Soviet advisers, a mutual defense treaty, and other specific forms of large-scale cooperation ensued in short order. This condition lasted for about a decade. But by the early 1960's,

Peking had begun to lean away from Moscow — though pointedly not in the direction of Washington!

Two events of 1965–1966, only half a year apart, reveal how far relations between the two giants of Communism have deteriorated. The first was a major policy pronouncement by Chinese Communist Defense Minister Lin Piao in September 1965. In this document, which was published in all official Chinese Communist organs and broadcast abroad, the Soviet Union is branded as a "betrayer of people's war" and the Kremlin is accused of "working hand in glove with the U.S. imperialists." Moreover, Lin's statement of Chinese Communist plans for the world is scarcely calculated to create anything but apprehension in Moscow or in Washington. The most significant policy pronouncement to come out of Peking in two decades, the document sounds disturbingly like a kind of *Mein Kampf*. In effect, Peking serves notice on the Kremlin of Communist China's intention to go it alone and aggressive! After reaffirming the correctness of the Maoist strategy of the revolutionary base in the rural area, Lin says: "Taking the entire globe, if North America and Western Europe can be called 'the cities of the world,' then Asia, Africa, and Latin America constitute 'the rural areas of the world.' " "In a sense," Lin concludes, "the whole cause of revolution hinges on the revolutionary struggles of the Asian, African, and Latin American peoples who make up the overwhelming majority of the world's population."

The second significant event occurred in the spring of 1966 when the Peking leadership announced its boycott of the 23rd Party Congress in Moscow. In declining the Moscow invitation, the Chinese Communists laid bare more of the nature and extent of Peking's bitterness. ". . . you sent an anti-Chinese letter to other Parties," Peking Radio ranted, "inciting them to join you in opposing China. You wantonly vilified the Chinese Party as being 'bellicose,' 'pseudo-revolutionary . . . encouraging U.S. imperialist aggression,' guilty of 'adventurism,' 'splittism,' 'Trotskyism,' 'nationalism,' 'great-power chauvinism,' 'dogmatism,' etc."

The blast went on to enumerate other unfraternal activities

and then concluded: "These anti-Chinese actions all go to show that your present invitation is merely a gesture and is sent with ulterior motives. In these circumstances, how can the Chinese Communist Party, which you look upon as an enemy, be expected to attend your congress?"

Whether the "anti-Chinese letter" is a genuine article or a phoney document is perhaps less important than the impact the document was bound to have on Soviet-Chinese relations. And for good reason! Consider, for example, some of the comments contained in the alleged letter, a partial text of which was published in the West German daily *Die Welt* (Hamburg) on March 21, 1966.

"The Chinese people are made to believe the Soviet Union is their main enemy."

"... the Chinese side is provoking border conflicts."

"... the Chinese leaders are directing their foreign policy not so much against imperialist states as against the Soviet Union ..."

"... the Chinese leaders have set up fractional groups in about 30 countries [and are] ... openly interfering with the domestic affairs of other Communist parties."

"The course toward socialist revolution ... has been replaced by the course toward a world war ..."

These are only a few of the points made in the alleged letter, the authenticity of which Moscow has neither confirmed nor denied. Whatever the case, the fraternal relations between the two Communist powers seem clearly on the rocks.

A capsule review of the postwar Soviet and Chinese Communist press highlights the ten-year process of the disaffection and reveals the public about-face made by both powers. In the early 1950's, Mao Tse-tung repeatedly spoke "with love" of the Soviet Union and advised that China must "learn from the Soviet Union on a nation-wide scale." "The Soviet Union," he said, "is always with China, in joy and in sorrows."

By the early 1960's, Mao was attacking the Soviet Union and openly branding its leaders as "modern revisionists" who proceed from "absurd arguments" on the world situation and on

Marxism-Leninism. Khrushchev, Mao added, is a "Bible-reading and psalm-singing buffoon . . . a laughing stock." The Soviets now began to attack China openly and to engage in a bit of personal invective themselves: "Mao," Khrushchev retorted, is "a man old but not wise, who reminds one of a worn-out galosh which can only be put in a corner of a room to be admired." The "fraternal exchange," as we have seen, continues in the press of both countries; the issue by 1966 had become embarrassingly public. That the dispute is rooted in more than a huge personality clash may be established by the fact that the political demise of Khrushchev in 1964 has done nothing to heal the open breach. Indeed, in the Brezhnev-Kosygin years since, relations between Moscow and Peking have, if anything, worsened.

How deep is the rift between the Soviet Union and Communist China? What are its root causes? What are the implications for the Communist world and for us?

I

Russia is Russia and China is China. This seemingly obvious point is worth pondering briefly because it does serve to explain a critical aspect of Moscow-Peking disaffection. Three fundamental differences between Russia as Russia and China as China, quite apart from communism, make up the ocean of discontent on which the waves of mutual malice ebb and flow. Not that nationalism is necessarily always the controlling factor; but it is there, and both the Russians and the Chinese talk as much about country as about communism.

What is this ocean of discontent? What are its three principal ingredients?

The first is the difference in historical traditions and cultural heritage. Power, arrogance, expansionism, and distrust of anything foreign have all characterized China throughout her history. From the dawn of civilization well into the modern period, China was the recognized leader of Asia. Areas on the periphery of Asia, including Japan, acknowledged their linguistic, cultural, religious, artistic, and literary indebtedness to China. China regarded herself proudly as the Middle Kingdom — the center of the universe. This pride in her heritage has caused China to adopt an increasingly nationalistic attitude. Everywhere in the Communist world, "This is my own, my native land," has shown itself to be a feeling at least as strong as, if not noticeably more powerful than, the slogan "Workers of the world, unite!"

The second is the difference in experience with the West. Long experience with Western imperialism has left an indelible mark on China. "Unequal treaties," "gunboat diplomacy," "treaty ports," "international settlements," "second-rate citizen" — these are all terms which conjure up bitter memories in the minds of the Chinese. These terms are largely meaningless to most Russians. Russia has simply not been the target of the kind of Western imperialism imposed upon certain areas of China during the nineteenth century. Thus, the Chinese Communists can reinforce Marxist-Leninist slogans with a long and impressive list of specific grievances against the West.

The third is the difference in level of economic development. China is a "have-not" nation. The U.S.S.R. is relatively a "have" nation. If there is still imbalance between Soviet industry and agriculture, there is far less than in China, and the imbalance in Russia is somewhat corrected by the extensive foreign trade of the U.S.S.R. Steel production in Communist China last year, for example, was only about one-sixth of that in the U.S.S.R., but China's exploding population of some 700 million people already outnumbers that of Russia by more than three to one.

Realizing that the development of an industrial base would have to have a parallel development in agriculture, Chinese Communists introduced the communes in 1958; by the early 1960's the communes had proved largely unworkable and were, accordingly, quietly modified. Despite having patterned the basic economy after the Soviet model, Communist China has nevertheless developed economic, political, administrative, military, and party organizations and practices that differ from those organizations which are found in the Soviet Union. The point is that the leaders in Peking appear painfully conscious of China's economic inferiority.

There are, of course, other differences, but these three are basic and, as we shall see, excruciatingly relevant. Indeed, without them and the "ocean of discontent" which they feed, it is doubtful that the "waves of malice" would be as towering as they are or the issues and specific grievances between Moscow and Peking so critical and difficult to resolve.

II

As to the specific issues which divide Moscow and Peking, the ideological issue must be put first, if only because that is what both Moscow and Peking claim the whole dispute is all about. Actually, the specific grievances go far beyond ideology, as has already been suggested. But — let us make no mistake about it — ideology *is* important, and the differences over theory are basic. They are two in number. One has to do with the "path to socialism," a sacred Communist concept which prescribes the course from purgatory to paradise. Moscow says Marx's prescription was correct; Peking insists that Mao's ideas are more up-to-date than Moscow's. The issue relates to the stages through which society must pass, with the Kremlin claiming (à la Marx) that the stage of industrial society must precede socialism, which in turn can only at that point be converted to communism. Mao and company take the position that the developing nations can skip the totally industrialized stage and still achieve communism — or at least Maoism. In 1957, Mao put forward a new approach, the commune system, those huge army camplike centers which Peking bragged "already contain the shoots of pure communism." Khrushchev commented in 1958 that Mao's idea was unworkable, nonsense, and that the Soviets had tried the idea in the 1920's and found that it did not work.

In early July 1963, in an open letter, the Central Committee of the Communist Party of the Soviet Union attacked the Chinese Communist Party leaders for suggesting that Soviet society had gone soft on capitalism, was being "bourgeoisified," was "degenerating." "According to such logic," the document said, "if people wear bast [coarse fiber] sandals and eat thin soup from a common bowl — that is communism, and if a working man lives well and wants to live better still tomorrow — that is nearly the restoration of capitalism. And this," the letter concluded, "is the philosophy they [the leaders of Communist China] want to present to us as the latest revelation of Marxism-Leninism!"

The other ideological difference is over the question of coexistence. The Soviets are for it; the Chinese Communists are not. Does the Kremlin really believe in coexistence or is this one more Communist deception? The answer is that the leaders in Moscow are, indeed, serious in their advocacy of coexistence. But it is important to make clear what the Kremlin means when it speaks of coexistence. By coexistence the Soviets mean the absence of nuclear war — no more, no less. They clearly do not mean genuine, lasting cooperation with the West, nor has anyone in authority in Moscow suggested that the Soviets have abandoned their fundamental Marxist-Leninist assumptions and objective — control of the world. Brezhnev put it this way in *Pravda* in March 1965 when he said: "The Soviet Union firmly supports the Leninist course of peaceful coexistence of states with different social systems. This suits the vital interests of all peoples, since in today's conditions it is the only way to spare mankind the calamities of a world nuclear war."

III

A second major area of disenchantment and apprehension is the issue of Soviet-Chinese Communist military relations. Peking clearly feels "let down" by Moscow. The Kremlin, for its part, has shown itself more than reluctant to see nuclear weapons in the hands of so arrogant and inscrutable an ally.

From the Peking perspective, the problem has two fairly distinct aspects: (a) dissatisfaction over the nature and scope of conventional military assistance and support, and (b) resentment over the Soviet refusal to share nuclear know-how and nuclear weapons with her Asian ally.

The conspicuous characteristic of Soviet conventional military aid to Communist China over the past decade and a half is that it has been focused on tactical rather than strategic capabilities: fighter aircraft rather than long-range bombers; tanks rather than submarines (the Soviets are thought to have provided Communist China with some twenty older-model submarines); surface-to-air, but no long-range missiles. Two further limitations on independent Chinese Communist conventional capabilities relate to the apparent lack of spare parts for Soviet-built aircraft and the refusal of the Kremlin to provide the Chinese Communists with their own domestic jet fuel production facilities. Taken together, these last two items must raise serious political as well as military questions in Peking. Is Moscow using such devices in order to keep ultimate control of the Chinese Communist war machine?

Moreover, aside from Korea, where the issue is still unclear, the Soviets have shown little enthusiasm or support for Chinese Communist military adventures beyond the mainland Chinese borders. In the matter of the projected "liberation of Taiwan," and notably in the Quemoy and Matsu islands crisis of several years ago, there is reason to suspect that Moscow may have exercised a restraining influence. Certainly, in the case of the Chinese Communist military intrusion into India, the Soviet Union backed India with both words and deeds to the extent of supplying India with production facilities for first-line Soviet jet aircraft, a plant now nearing completion.

Moscow quite apparently regards Peking's approach to nuclear matters as immature and irresponsible, not to say insulting. Speaking before the Central Committee (Feb. 14, 1964), Presidium member and policy planner M. A. Suslov said: "It is well known that the leaders of the People's Republic of

China insistently sought to obtain the atomic bomb from the Soviet Union. They expressed their deep mortification when our country did not give them samples of nuclear weapons. . . . In a fit of irritation," Suslov concluded, "the CPC leaders went so far as to say that the threat of a nuclear war comes not from imperialism but from the 'modern revisionists,' unambiguously hinting at the Soviet Union . . ."

After the explosion of the first of several Chinese Communist atomic or nuclear devices, Peking asserted that Communist China would have accomplished the feat sooner except for Soviet "sabotage." During the early honeymoon years, Moscow did assist China for a time in this critical field. A number of Chinese scientists went to the Soviet Union for training in nuclear technology at a Joint Institute on Nuclear Research established in Moscow in 1956. By late 1960, the Chairman of the Chinese People's Republic could boast that China had four nuclear reactors that could be converted to military uses. Moscow is thought to have supplied Peking with a small amount of Uranium 234. But such cooperation ended abruptly as Moscow-Peking relations began to deteriorate. As early as 1963, alluding to Peking's persistent claim that thermonuclear weapons are a "paper tiger" which need not be feared, Soviet Marshal A. Yeremenko said that Peking's idea of destroying imperialism with atomic bombs in order to "enable mankind to build a civilization a thousand times more beautiful" is dangerous nonsense. "Whoever is hunting for tigers," he warned, "must be aware of the teeth and nails of this wild beast." Then he added, "We would advise the Peking 'theoreticians' that before speaking in such a casual manner about thermonuclear arms, they should evaluate the already universally known facts on the truly horrible consequences of the use of such arms . . ."

How far Soviet-Chinese military relations have deteriorated may be judged by a few of the statements made by Foreign Minister Chen Yi on July 10, 1966. Addressing a rally in Peking held to denounce U.S. policy in Vietnam, Chen used the occasion to brand the Soviet Union an "ignominious accomplice" of the United States and to charge Moscow with "military deployment along the Chinese border in coordination with the U.S. imperialist encirclement of China." Chen also accused the Soviet leaders of hypocrisies with respect to Vietnam and of "spreading lies and slanders everywhere by accusing China of obstructing the transit of aid materials to Vietnam." Chen concluded: "The facts are very clear. The Soviet revisionist clique is redoubling its efforts to take 'united action' with U.S. imperialism in a big way in order to sabotage the revolutionary peoples of the world."

IV

A third major problem area between Moscow and Peking is the issue of economic relations. This issue has been intensified and exacerbated by the fact that the Chinese Communist economy has been in serious difficulty, on and off, ever since the Communist regime came to power in Peking in October 1949. Both the backyard furnaces and the commune system — the twin "plans" designed by Mao to improve or supplement Communist China's industrial and agricultural sectors — have proved to be dismal failures.

The evidence attesting to Communist China's economic distress comes from several sources: The secret Chinese Communist military documents which fell into American hands in 1961; interviews with refugees from mainland China who have fled by the thousands into Hong Kong; the Chinese Communists' own statements.

Information on the Chinese Communist military documents was originally released by the Department of State on August 5, 1963. A huge 776-page tome containing the full translation, edited by J. Chester Cheng, of the "Activities of the People's Liberation Army" was published by the Hoover Institution in 1966. Twenty-nine issues of the secret Chinese Red Army military journal (Jan. 1 through Aug. 26, 1961) are included; they reveal the seriousness of the economic and social problems besetting China. Typical excerpts from these documents: "In our economic eye . . . this year we suffered calamities greater than any during the last hundred years." (Secret — "Directive, Army Units Stationed in Seriously Affected Disaster Areas and of Those Whose Families are in Disaster Areas.") Another, "Report on the Entire Army's Large-Scale Movement for Production of Substitute Food," suggests the seriousness of the problem: ". . . substitute food," it says, "not only has economic value, but can be used to feed both human beings and pigs . . ." Still another document reports (Feb. 25, 1961): ". . . the conditions of those who suffered from edema throughout the Army are more serious than we previously realized . . . emergency measures must be taken." The cause of the problem, according to the document, "lies mainly in the poor conditions of livelihood giving rise to undernourishment."

Chinese refugees with whom I have talked in Hong Kong on several occasions in the years 1962 through 1965, as well as reports of others interviewed, confirm serious economic conditions in various parts of south China. Several refugees among the flood of more than 50,000 which in the summer of 1962 threatened to inundate already overcrowded Hong Kong, spoke, for example, of not having seen any meat in the shops of Canton and other cities of China for many months. Others outlined the desperate food situation in the countryside. Typical of comments from these refugees is the revelation of a simple Chinese farm woman who said to me: "We don't see any Russian goods in our stores, but we know that the prize hogs from China are shipped off to the Soviet Union to be eaten by the Russians."

These same escapees and those who came later told of indoctrination lectures in which Party cadre members, dispatched from Peking, placed the blame for China's economic woes on broken Soviet promises and the lack of adequate aid from the Soviet Union. Thus, at the rice-roots level, the Chinese economic problem is rationalized and explained as stemming from bad faith in Moscow rather than bad planning in Peking. Unseasonable weather and/or a poor harvest are also arguments regularly employed by Peking to justify why, after so many years of Communist control and extravagant promises, life is still so severe.

What are the specific points of issue, the grudging grievances between Moscow and Peking in the economic realm? At least four may be worth noting. First, Peking appears to be terribly unhappy over Soviet aid to India, Egypt, and other non-Communist nations. Peking asks: Why should a Soviet steel mill go to India or a Soviet generator plant to Egypt, or elsewhere, when China is in need? The traditional Chinese emphasis on the importance of the family apparently has its international dimension. Second, the withdrawal by Moscow of some 13,000 Soviet advisers who had come to China during the 1950's was, Peking insists, deliberately designed to slow down the pace of Chinese Communist economic development. Moscow replies that, quite to the contrary, the Soviet advisers were "asked to leave" by the Chinese Communist authorities by whom, it is suggested, they had never been treated with the respect to which they were accustomed.

Third is the matter of the terms of Soviet assistance. Peking obviously resents the fact that Moscow prefers loans rather than aid to China — loans which Peking is even now obliged to pay off. This practice, it may be noted, is a standard Soviet policy, and China, apparently, is no exception — and that is, perhaps, the point. Finally, there is the question of Soviet and Chinese economic competition in Africa, Asia, and the Middle East. This has taken the form of two different approaches to the developmental questions of the underdeveloped or developing countries, with Peking suggesting that these nations study the thought of Mao Tse-tung in order better to "do it themselves." Moscow, of course, is willing *and able* to provide some of the specific equipment and commodity needs of the new nations. Thus economic gamesmanship looking toward political advantage goes on in the Communist world with the result of increasing the bitterness between the Soviet Union and Communist China.

V

The issue between Moscow and Peking which is clearly the most upsetting to the Kremlin is the Chinese Communist attempt to muscle in on the "international Communist movement." For some four decades this had been a sacred and significant Moscow preserve. Communist parties throughout the world pledged their allegiance to the Union of Soviet Socialist Republics and were obliged by statute to defend the Soviet Union. The Kremlin thus had, in the form of Communist parties in most of the nations of the world, a huge, built-in volunteer and low-cost communications, influence, propaganda, and espionage apparatus of enormous value. In practice this meant that any world-wide policy put forward by Moscow immediately became binding on, and a crash program of, the individual Communist parties of the world. During the 1920's and the early 1930's relations with the Communist parties in Europe, Asia, America, and elsewhere were handled largely through the Comintern. Later, Moscow increasingly took over the task directly. But in both cases, the subservience of the foreign Communist parties to Moscow "guidance" is an established, historical fact.

With the emergence of a second major nation under communism, this pattern, like so many other things in the world of communism, began gradually to change. Even before the Communists came to power in Peking, they had their own separate lines to several of the Asian Communist parties, notably the parties in Malaya, Indonesia, and the Philippines. The millions of overseas Chinese, largely in Asia, obviously constituted a huge potential asset which Peking has regularly sought to exploit by all manner of inducement and intimidation. With the achievement of national power which included recognition by many nations, the Peking leadership began increasingly to make its world-wide influence felt as far as Eastern Europe. Pro-Peking Albania soon became the thermometer of Soviet-Chinese relations. Other parties, such as the Japanese

Communist Party, jumped on the Peking bandwagon, and by the 23rd Soviet Party Congress in 1966, even the New Zealand party had aligned itself publicly with Communist China in refusing to attend the Congress in Moscow.

Again, M. A. Suslov was called upon by the Central Committee of the CPSU to put the issue squarely. He did. "The Chinese leaders," he said, "pretend that the interests of the peoples of Asia, Africa, and Latin America are particularly near and dear to them and that they are concerned above all else with the further progress of the national liberation movement. The CPC leadership," he concluded, "is clearly trying to establish control over the national liberation struggle in order to make it an instrument for the implementation of its hegemonic plans."

VI

Finally, two sizzling issues between Moscow and Peking are the territorial and the racial questions. These have all the earmarks of the kinds of matters usually associated solely with the "imperialist powers." This perhaps makes the questions all the more delicate and damaging.

Moscow has charged the Peking government with several thousand separate violations of Soviet territory along the world's longest and most poorly defined frontier, which runs from Siberia in the north down through Central Asia to the Turkestan approaches to India and Pakistan.

The population density and population explosion in Communist China are reason enough to give the policy planners in Moscow cause for concern. The present population of China is estimated to be about 700 million and increasing at the rate of more than ten million per year.

A story circulating in Moscow tells of a Chinese Communist and a Soviet diplomat exchanging views at a reception in Peking. The Chinese comrade is supposed to have asked: "Why don't you Russians permit us Chinese to resettle a certain number of Chinese in the sparsely settled regions of Siberia beyond China's borders, thus helping us solve our population problem?" The Russian is represented as having replied: "What do you mean by a certain number?" The Chinese response: "Oh, say ninety or a hundred million!"

The Kremlin is clearly concerned over Chinese intrusion into areas which have historically been regarded as Soviet preserves if not outright Soviet territory.

A final, almost unbelievable issue between the two major centers of Communist power is the racial issue — unbelievable if only because from the dawn of modern communism a basic tenet has always been that race is unimportant, that creed is all that matters. Anyone, whatever the color of his skin — white, black, yellow, or red, so the doctrine preaches — can become a top Communist so long as he acknowledges his faith in Marxism-Leninism and proves himself loyal to the Party.

In article after article, Peking complains about the Soviet leaders having "taken over the racial superiority complex of the European and American bourgeoisie . . ." Moscow is not qualified to guide Africa and Asia, we are told, because:

"Although two-thirds of Soviet territory is in Asia, almost three-fourths of its population is in Europe. Its political centre all along has been in Europe. Traditionally, it is a European country" (*Peking Review*, June 25, 1965).

What could be further from orthodox Marxist-Leninist theory than representatives of Communist China appearing in Africa to advise the Africans to follow Peking's lead "in the ideological dispute with Moscow"? Why? Not only because of the superiority of the thought of Mao Tse-tung but because, the Chinese Communists announced, "We, like you in Africa, are members of the colored race."

This provoked an immediate and indignant response from the Kremlin which ended with the neat Soviet editorial comment: "We trust we are not about to witness the return of the Yellow Peril."

Upon his visit to Communist China in the fall of 1965, Cambodian head of state Prince Norodom Sihanouk commented on the Sino-Soviet dispute as follows: "This is simply a manifestation of racism," he said. "The Russians are drawing closer to the Americans because, like them, they are white. To them, the 'yellow peril' refers above all to China, and those who are friends of the Chinese are their [the Russians'] enemies."

VII

What is the balance sheet? The implications? The projection?

Any way one looks at it, it does not seem likely that Moscow and Peking will be able to resolve their basic differences in the foreseeable future. Even though Brezhnev and Kosygin may continue in their attempts to paper things over, the issues between the two countries are too fundamental, the hurt too deep. Nor would the death of Mao Tse-tung — any more than the recent political demise of Khrushchev — be likely to erase the many-sided and deep-seated antagonism between the two Communist giants. It is of course possible, perhaps even to be expected, that the coming years will see the lessening on both sides of the intensity of public debate. It is even conceivable that in several areas of mutual advantage, a façade of unity may emerge. But this is something quite different from suggesting the prospects of rapprochement.

For the Soviet Union this would seem to imply a continuing competition for the loyalties of the 87 Communist parties of the world. It also must mean more economic gamesmanship in the areas of Africa, Asia, the Middle East, and perhaps Latin America. Further, the external effort to "purify" Marxist-Leninist theory and to settle on a single, universally acceptable doctrine for the faithful is likely to remain as far from realization as at any time in the history of communism.

Peking, for its part, can scarcely assume that the Soviet Union would come to its aid (treaty or not) should Communist China get itself involved in a conflict with the United States. This, obviously, makes a substantial difference in the do's and don't's of international behavior. For the foreseeable future, then, Peking is likely to speak loudly, but carry a small stick.

This is to assume, as I do, that the Communist leaders in Peking are rational beings who really are not anxious to see the total destruction of the industrial and military complex of Communist China.

It is conceivable, but not likely, that Peking may overplay its hand. The parallel of the Korean war has been suggested. This would seem to be a poor analogy. The three most obvious and critical differences between the situation then in Korea and now in Vietnam are: (1) the difference in the status of Peking's relationship with Moscow, (2) the difference arising out of Korea's strategic location vis-à-vis the industrial heartland of China, and (3) the difference in United States policy, forces-in-being, and resolve.

This leads me to two final conclusions: First, that the emergence of China as a second, aggressive Communist power center in Asia confronts the United States with two arrogant enemies instead of one. This is to suggest that, until we have specific evidence of the abandonment by Moscow of its Marxist-Leninist objectives, we would do well not to overrate the progress toward détente or to underrate the element of ideology, right along with nationalism and power. In short, we should continue to hope, and work, for the best — but prepare for the worst. I do not mean to imply that a nuclear war or, for that matter, an all-out war between East and West fought with conventional weapons is inevitable or even likely. Quite to the contrary, it seems to me increasingly *unlikely*, if only for the simple reason that great powers throughout history have seldom willfully indulged in certain mutual self-destruction.

Second, the Soviet policy of "peaceful coexistence" must be viewed realistically and in context and perspective. To be sure, the several recent indicators of a somewhat more mellow and reasonable line on the part of the Kremlin are encouraging. Still, I see no fundamental change in Soviet foreign policy objectives and precious few indications of a willingness on the part of the Soviet leaders to settle, except on exclusively Soviet terms, any of the basic issues which divide the Communist and non-Communist worlds. Nor does it necessarily follow that because the Kremlin has deep-seated problems with China, the Soviet leadership will establish a new kind of long-lasting friendship with the United States. After all, we do have some past experience with those earlier periods of coexistence — the NEP (1921–1927), the United Front (1934–1939), and the wartime era (1941–1945).

Perhaps this time, with Communist China in the picture, things will be different. It is to be hoped that relations with the Soviet Union will continue to improve. Certainly, we should encourage the process by whatever means consistent with national security. But until the character and amount of evidence of such a change in Soviet foreign policy — not to mention that of Communist China — is somewhat more substantial, we should perhaps heed the caution of a British colleague: "We must beware," he said, "of mistaking a change in the weather for a change in the climate."

INDEX